A [illegible]

Besides being the smallest [illegible] only one who wore short trousers, Brock was almost the only boy without a bike. He'd seemed to be wanting one all his life, and now on his eleventh birthday he was sure he really would get one and that it would be just the sort he wanted, a real racing bike, quick and light to handle and smart to look at.

But it was a disaster. An upright Army surplus machine, as heavy as a tank and requiring superhuman strength to pedal it. It was the most crushing disappointment of Brock's life, and made worse by the jokes his gang were cracking about him and the bike, but Brock was determined to fight the humiliation in his own way. *Somehow*, he vowed, he would earn the money to buy the bike of his dreams, and he wouldn't be long about it.

RICHARD POTTS

A Boy and His Bike

Illustrated by Charles Keeping

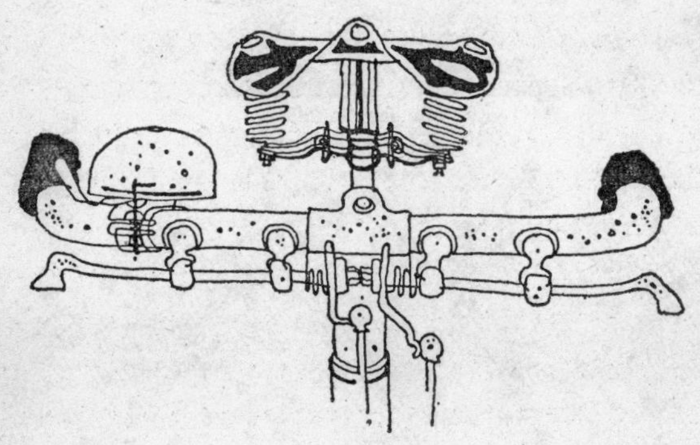

PUFFIN BOOKS

Puffin Books, Penguin Books Ltd, Harmondsworth, Middlesex, England
Penguin Books, 625 Madison Avenue, New York, New York 10022, U.S.A.
Penguin Books Australia Ltd, Ringwood, Victoria, Australia
Penguin Books Canada Ltd, 2801 John Street, Markham, Ontario, Canada L3R 1B4
Penguin Books (N.Z.) Ltd, 182–190 Wairau Road, Auckland 10, New Zealand

First published by Dobson Books Ltd 1976
Published in Puffin Books 1979

Made and printed in Great Britain
by Richard Clay (The Chaucer Press), Ltd,
Bungay, Suffolk
Set in Linotype Pilgrim

For
Anna and Kirsty and Kathleen
and for
Charles Keeping,
a fine artist and a good friend

ANNOUNCING
THE
PARIS
Tourmaster
SUN
THE 1975
CHAMPION
Tour
Get a
C.F.H

One

Brock, whose real name was John Brockson, had a round moon-like face, and his blond hair, which was almost white, fell down over his ears. He was the smallest boy in his class, and he was the only one who hadn't a pair of long trousers. Brock would have liked long trousers, but much more than that, he yearned for a bike. He had yearned for years and years, and now that his eleventh birthday was approaching, Dad couldn't say no. It was agreed that Brock should have a bike on his birthday, the 22nd of July. That was the first day of the summer holidays.

Brock went to every cycle shop in town. He wrote all the prices in a notebook and he kept showing it to his mum. At one shop a man gave him four bike posters, which Brock pinned to his bedroom wall. Mum wouldn't agree to any of the bikes, but he persuaded her to meet him after school in town, the Monday afternoon before his birthday.

Brock was out of school that day before the bell

had stopped ringing. He met Mum in the café opposite the station. She was sitting by the window and Brock waved to her as he ran across the square. She was small like Brock, but her hair was dark and it was peppered with strands of white.

'Did you have a nice day at school?' she asked him.

'Yes, thank you,' Brock answered absently. His mind was on the cycle shops.

'Well, aren't you going to sit down while I finish my coffee?' she went on. Brock dropped into a chair on the other side of the table.

'You can have a drink if you would like one,' Mum said.

'No, thank you,' Brock told her.

'Are you nearly ready?' he asked impatiently. Mum placed the cup on its saucer and glanced up at the station clock.

'Just look at the time,' she said. 'And I haven't bought Mollie her fish yet.' Mollie was their ginger cat.

'We can do that later,' Brock said. 'Only let's go to my cycle shops first.'

He stood up and lifted her shopping bag from beside her chair.

'We really ought to leave it till another day,' Mum told him. 'Dad will be home soon and you know how annoyed he is when tea isn't ready on time.'

'But you promised,' Brock accused. 'You gave me your word.' Mum didn't answer. She took a fifty pence piece from her purse and walked to the cash desk. Brock waited for her at the door.

'There's one on the other side of the station,' Brock explained, as they walked into the street. 'It'll only take a few minutes.'

'I suppose so,' Mum agreed, with a sigh and a smile. Brock smiled back at her. 'You wait and see,' he told her. 'They've got exactly what I want.'

The rush-hour traffic had started already, though it was only half past four. It took them almost five minutes to cross the square. Brock hurried on in front. Once he lost Mum in the crowds and had to go back for her. The cycle shop behind the station was not the one he had intended Mum to see. It didn't have many racing-bikes for a start, and in addition nothing there was very cheap. Still, in the circumstances, he had been lucky to make her change her mind.

The bell jangled as Brock opened the door. It was quiet and still inside the shop after the bustle and noise of the street.

'Can I help you, Madam?' the server said.

'We'd like to look around for ourselves if we may,' Mum told him.

'Most certainly,' the man answered, stepping back to the counter. He folded his arms and watched them, as Brock led Mum between the cycles, which hung suspended from the ceiling.

'It's terribly expensive in here, John,' Mum whispered, holding up a label which read £69·50.

'This one's only £52,' Brock said, pointing to a lightweight silver racing-bike with low alloy handlebars and a slim leather saddle. Mum held the ticket between her fingers. She seemed to deliberate.

'Can I have this one?' Brock pleaded. Mum hesitated and didn't answer.

'I'll put all my own money towards it,' Brock said eagerly. For more than a year he'd been saving for a bike. He had five pounds and fifteen pence in his piggy-bank.

'I really honestly don't know,' Mum said. 'Perhaps – we'll – we'll have to see – we'll need to speak to your father about it when we get home.'

'This is a first-class model,' the man broke in, approaching them. He must have been listening to their conversation. 'My own son has one so I can recommend it from personal experience.'

'Don't you think it's perfect, Mum?'

'Would you like me to take it down for you, Madam?'

'No, that won't be necessary,' Mum answered firmly.

'I can assure you, it isn't any trouble.'

'No, thank you,' Mum said curtly. 'We really

must go.' She turned and picked up her shopping bag from the floor.

'Come on, John,' she said. 'Or we'll never get home.' The man moved in front of them and held open the door.

Brock reluctantly followed Mum out into the street. The pavements were teeming with people, and the noise was deafening. It took them ages to return to the station, and then all their buses were full. They had to take one which went to the far side of the estate, and that meant a walk of almost a mile.

When they finally did reach home, Mollie was miaowing at the kitchen door to be let in, and Dad was sitting in his armchair reading the evening newspaper. Brock knew from the expression on his face that Dad was not very pleased.

'I was wondering what had happened to you two,' he said gloomily.

'Town was so busy,' Mum explained. 'And John wanted to show me some bikes.'

'Oh! Did he!' Dad said, raising his bushy eyebrows. He gave a dissatisfied grunt, and then returned to his newspaper.

Brock followed Mum into the kitchen. Mollie jumped onto the draining-board. She rubbed her face into Mum's jumper and made loud purring noises.

'Look at that poor cat,' Mum said. 'She'll just

have to make do with the scraps.' Mum went into the pantry and came out with three eggs. She nearly fell over Mollie as she reached for a saucepan.

'Don't just stand there, John,' she snapped. 'Go and lay the table – now there's a good boy.'

Brock collected everything onto the tray and carried it through into the dining-room. Dad glanced up and fingered the ends of his moustache. He turned the pages of the newspaper and went on reading. After Brock had laid the table he switched on the television. As sounds of shouts and screams filled the room, Dad lowered his newspaper and glared.

'Would you mind turning that noise down,' he said sharply. Brock went to the set and adjusted the volume control.

'Thank you,' Dad said, and then he continued reading. Brock sat on the edge of the settee. As he did so the picture appeared on the screen. It was a serial about King Arthur and the Knights of the Round Table. Brock had watched it before. After a minute he tried the other channels, but there was nothing interesting, so he switched off altogether. He could see that Dad wanted the room to be quiet.

Brock was about to see how long tea would be when Dad neatly folded the newspaper, placed it on the arm of his chair and then stood up. Brock always felt dwarfed beside his dad.

'Don't go away,' Dad said. 'I'd like a word with you.' He went over to his bureau by the window, and took a magazine from one of the drawers. The back page was full of advertisements. One of the advertisements had a ring drawn round it in thick black pencil.

'Perhaps I ought not to tell you this before Saturday,' Dad said very seriously, passing a hand over his balding head. 'But I can see you've been bothering your mother, so I think we ought to be clear about the sort of bike you are to have for your birthday.'

Brock felt his heart beat quicker as he took the magazine from Dad's outstretched hand. Then he wasn't to have a racing-bike after all. Mum must have known all along, yet she'd let him take her to the cycle shop and she hadn't said a word. Brock read inside the circle of black pencil.

CYCLES FOR SALE AND WANTED

COVENTRY Eagle Flight De Luxe 5-speed Racer, £15. — Tel. Elvington 315462.

GIRL'S CYCLE. Suit 8-11 years. Excellent condition. £12. — Phone 66060.

STOP PRESS – SPECIAL OFFER British Army Cycles. Used but in excellent condition. Genuine Ex-Govt Surplus. From only £12.

That was all. There wasn't anything else, except the address. Nothing about what sort of bike it was.

'But I want a new bike,' Brock protested feebly. He was almost in tears. All the time, he had known deep down that he wouldn't have his racing-bike, but now facing the reality was too much for him.

'I've – I've been saving up,' Brock stuttered. 'Mum knows all about it. I've been showing her the bikes I want.' Instinctively he turned to Mum for support, but of course she wasn't there. Brock could hear her moving around in the kitchen.

'I know all about that,' Dad said, beginning to be annoyed.

'I've heard it from your mother already.' Dad paused and drew in a deep breath.

'Now this is a perfectly good bicycle,' he went on, stabbing his large thumb at the magazine. 'I rode one in the Army exactly like this. It's built to last, not like these modern contraptions. It'll take plenty of wear and tear. You wait and see for yourself.'

'But – I –' Brock began.

'Never mind about "buts",' Dad silenced him. 'Take my advice. Give this a try. If you find it's not what you want, then you can buy something for yourself in a year or two's time.'

'That's the tea ready,' Mum called. Dad sat down at the table, took the magazine from between Brock's fingers and placed it beside his plate.

'You'd better wash your hands,' Mum said, as

she came into the room. Brock obediently did as he was told. When he came downstairs Mum and Dad were eating their tea in silence. Brock sat in his chair and cracked the top of his egg. Mollie pushed open the door and miaowed at Mum.

'Hasn't that cat had its fish?' Dad asked angrily. Mum didn't answer. She picked Mollie up and pushed her back into the kitchen. They went on eating their eggs. Mum poured out the tea. She handed Dad his cup.

'Thank you, Mary,' Dad said. He added a spoonful of sugar and stirred thoughtfully. Taking a sip, he wiped a droplet of tea from his moustache.

'I've been telling John about his bike,' Dad said abruptly.

'I was hoping you would,' Mum answered. Brock stared at his plate.

'The more I think about it,' the more convinced I am this is the bicycle for our John,' Dad continued. 'While I was waiting for you I read about this boy involved in an accident. And it said he was riding one of these fast lightweight devices.'

'I'm sure you're right, Frank,' Mum told him.

Later that night Mum had a talk with Brock in his bedroom. She came to say good night as she did every evening.

'I shouldn't say anything else to Dad about your racing-bike,' Mum said in a low voice. 'There's been another awful day at the office, and Dad's terribly worried. Last week it was just the same. He hasn't had a proper night's sleep for I don't know how long. You must try and understand when he's upset like this. It isn't anything to do with you.' Mum gave Brock a knowing smile and Brock smiled faintly back at her.

'You take the bike and say no more. It's a bike and after all that's what matters. I'm sure it's quite nice, and it's certain to be very reliable and safe. Dad had one when he was in the Army so there can't be anything wrong with it.' Brock nodded his head as he looked into Mum's eyes. She smiled again, drew the curtains and kissed him good night.

On the Wednesday a postcard came to say that the bike had been delivered to the station. Dad went to fetch it that evening after Brock had gone to bed. He rode the bike home himself and locked it in the wash-house.

The following day Brock couldn't find the key anywhere, and when he peered through the wash-house window the bike was hidden from view. It was Thursday and Brock had two whole days to wait. He thought his birthday would never come.

Two

The moment Brock woke he remembered it was Saturday, that Saturday was his birthday, and the first day of the summer holidays. He lifted his wrist-watch to his face and saw it was twenty to eight. The post might have arrived.

He jumped out of bed and ran to the top of the stairway. There was only the newspaper on the carpet by the front door.

The postman probably hasn't reached here yet, Brock thought. At that very instant there was a knock at the door, Brock tore down the stairs, afraid the postman might not wait. 'Anything special today?' the man asked, as he handed him several letters and a parcel.

'Yes, it's my birthday,' Brock told him. He sat at the bottom of the stairs. There were six letters, four for him and two for Dad. He knew from the Irish stamps that the parcel was from Auntie Dot. Brock carried the letters and the parcel up-stairs.

Mum and Dad's door was half-open, so Brock

walked in. They were both still asleep. Mum was snuggled up onto Dad's shoulder, and Dad was lying on his back with his mouth slightly open. The alarm-clock on the dressing-table ticked noisily.

Brock backed away, but as he did so Mum rolled over. Her eyes opened and stared vacantly at Brock. For a fraction of a second she didn't recognize him. Then she saw the letters and smiled.

'Happy birthday, John,' she said. 'Are you going to sit here and open your letters?' As Brock sat beside her on the bed, the springs creaked beneath his weight. Dad gave a moan and buried his head in the pillow. Mum sat up and reached over to her bedside chair for a cardigan. She drew it round her shoulders. 'It is chilly these mornings,' she said. 'Aren't you cold?' Brock shook his head. He gave her Dad's two letters and she placed them on the pillow beside his ear. They both smiled together.

Brock opened his letters as quietly as he could, but the tearing paper seemed to make a terrible noise. Dad drew a hand over his face and opened his eyes.

'It's John's birthday, Frank,' Mum said.

'What – is it?' Dad groaned. 'Happy birthday, John.' Then he rolled to the far side of the bed, pulling the blankets after him.

Brock opened the rest of his letters and placed

the cards on the bedspread in front of Mum. There were postal orders from Granny and Grandad in London, Grandma in Scotland, and Auntie Margaret and Uncle Harold. Altogether they came to three pounds. Then there was a card from Brock's best friend Fagin, and one from Mum and Dad with a picture of a penny-farthing on the front of it. Mum had been hiding her card in her cardigan pocket.

'It took me all afternoon to find it,' Mum explained. That only left the parcel from Auntie Dot, which was a box of chocolates and another card. Brock opened the box and Mum and Brock chose a chocolate each.

Suddenly the alarm-clock rang.

'Look at the time, Mary,' Dad said, sitting up. It was five to eight.

'You climb into my bed until Daddy gets off to work,' Mum told Brock. 'Then you won't be in the way. And when you come down your bike will be ready for you.'

Brock climbed into Mum's side of the bed. He could feel the warmth where her body had been. While he was waiting he looked at his cards again and ate four more chocolates. And he counted his money. With his savings in his piggy-bank he had eight pounds and fifteen pence. That was a lot of money. In two years' time he would be able to buy a racing-bike for himself. But he hoped his birthday bike was all right. Two years was a long way off. Mum had said it was quite nice, though that was before the bike had arrived.

Brock heard the key turn in the wash-house. Dad was taking his bike out. Brock leapt out of bed and went into his own room. Mum had laid out his clothes on the chair. In less than a minute he was dressed.

Then the gate banged. Brock jumped down the stairs two at a time.

'There's a surprise for you in the yard,' Mum said, as he burst into the kitchen. Brock's heart was thumping when he followed her through the back door.

'Close your eyes,' Mum told him with a laugh. She took his hand and led him into the sunlight.

'You can open them now.'

Brock hadn't known what to expect but he hadn't anticipated what he saw in front of him. The bike was propped against the wash-house wall. The frame tubing was thick and it was painted a dull, dark brown colour. Everywhere else was black. In places the paint had cracked, revealing patches of red rust underneath. The handlebars were perfectly straight and at each end was a black rubber grip. The saddle was the broadest and the heaviest looking seat Brock had ever seen on a bike. It was adjusted to its lowest position. Tied to the brake-pipe was a card on which was printed:

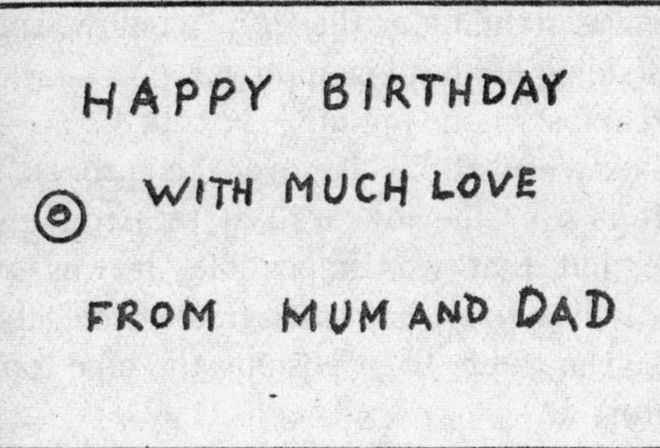

Brock knew Mum had done it by the small neat printing.

'Do you like it?' she asked him.

'I'm not sure,' Brock answered. He hesitated, not knowing what to say. Then he looked up and he saw the anxious expression on her face.

'It's really quite nice, I suppose,' he added.

'Have a ride and see what you think,' Mum told him. Brock nodded. He tried to smile, but really he felt hopeless. What would his friends say when they saw it? They'd make jokes and laugh at him about it.

Brock wheeled the bike through the gate onto the road. The frame was enormous and getting on was like mounting a horse. He wobbled along to the bottom of Churchill Street and then came back again. Fortunately the road was quiet so nobody saw him. Brock was glad because every time the bike went over a bump it made a clanging sound. Mum was standing at the front window, smiling and nodding her head in approval.

'Breakfast in one minute,' she called.

Brock wheeled the bike over the curb. He tried to lift it over the low wall at the front of the house, but that was impossible. It was so incredibly heavy. He had to reach over the gate and release the catch. Even pushing the bike took all his effort.

'Here you are,' Mum said. 'Your breakfast is all ready.' Brock followed her into the house.

'There's a grapefruit on the table for you,' Mum told him. 'I've given you a whole one because it's your birthday.' Grapefruit was Brock's favourite fruit. Brock sat down at the table and stirred his hot chocolate. Mum came in with two slices of toast.

'I've arranged your birthday cards for you,' Mum said, indicating the row of cards on the mantelshelf. Brock hadn't noticed them before. The one of the penny-farthing was the best.

'Have you any old cloths?' Brock asked. 'I want to clean my bike.'

'I'm sure I can find you something,' Mum said brightly. She came back a few minutes later with some torn-up rags and a tin of polish.

'I thought you might like this as well.'

'Yes, all right,' Brock answered. He drank the last of the hot chocolate and stood up.

'Now is there anything else, before I start work?' Mum asked.

'No, thank you.'

'Try and look a bit more cheerful,' Mum said. 'It is your birthday.' Brock nodded and walked past her into the back yard.

He spent the next two hours rubbing and polishing his bike. At the end it hardly looked any different than it had at the beginning. Brock threw the rag on the concrete and straightened his back. He had pins and needles in both legs and his fingers were red and raw from rubbing. It hurt him even to look at the bike. It was so cumbersome and ugly.

I wonder what Dad would say if I asked him to send it back, Brock thought.

He sat on the dustbin and half closed his eyes, but the bike was still just as terrible. It was while he was sitting there, that David Whitman, the boy from next door, jumped over the fence between the two houses. Whitman was fourteen and had curly red hair. He stared in astonishment at Brock's bike.

'Hello, Titch,' he said, coming closer. Whitman called Brock 'Titch' because he was so small. 'You don't mean to tell me this is your new bike!'

Brock didn't answer. He picked up a piece of rag and polished the rim on the front wheel.

'You're wasting your time cleaning that,' Whitman said scornfully.

Whitman built his own racing-bikes. Only last week he'd finished building another one. Whitman collected all the parts and then put them together himself. He was really brilliant at it. He sold the last bike for thirty pounds. And he only had it a few weeks before he found a buyer. The one he'd just built was in his wash-house. It was white all over except for the alloy parts. A boy named Brian Anderson called the day it was finished. He offered twenty-two pounds, but Whitman said he wasn't taking a penny less than thirty. Brock would have given anything for a bike like that.

Brock added some more polish to the rag and started on the handlebars.

'Come out of there,' Whitman told him, pushing Brock to one side. He lifted the bike with one hand, held it still, groaned and then pretended to collapse beneath the weight.

'Where did it come from?' he demanded, shaking the bike so it made loud rattling sounds.

'My dad bought it from the army,' Brock explained. He wished Whitman would go away and leave him alone.

'It looks like it,' Whitman said, laughing sarcastically. 'They must have used it for a tank before they sent it to you.'

He turned the bike upside down and laid it on the concrete path.

'The chain's too slack,' he observed grimly. 'And this frame's buckled by the appearance of things.' He wiped his hands disdainfully on a piece of rag. Then without asking permission, he carried the bike into the street and rode away on it.

Mum came rushing out of the front door, her hands covered in flour. She was terribly upset.

'You shouldn't have let that boy ride your bike,' Mum said in an agitated voice. 'What do you think Dad will say if he damages it!'

'It won't happen again,' Brock promised. He felt completely defeated. Mum looked anxiously down the road, wiped her hands on her apron, and then went back into the house. Brock sat on the edge of the curb and drew an outline of a racing-bike in the dirt with the end of a sharp stone.

Five minutes later, when Whitman rode back up the street, there was an expression of disgust on his face. He was breathing hard and beads of sweat stood out on his forehead. He lifted the bike over the wall and dropped it on the yard, as if it was a sack of coal. Then he stood, staring at the bike, slowly shaking his head.

'How much did you say your Dad paid?' he asked.

'Twelve pounds,' Brock told him.

'Twelve pounds,' Whitman repeated with an astonished whistle. 'He was robbed – must have been out of his mind. I wouldn't give you twelve pence for it. It's worse than your dad's horse and that's saying a lot.'

Brock turned away, deeply hurt. To hide his feelings he began to collect the rags together. One piece had blown almost into the next garden. When Brock went to fetch it he saw Whitman's Dad planting some flowers. He must have heard the whole conversation.

Brock screwed the cap on the polish and at that moment a window above them was noisily opened. Peter, Whitman's six-year-old brother leaned out.

'Mummy says dinner is ready,' Peter called. 'She says you've to come this minute.'

'Those are my orders,' Whitman said. 'I'll have to make a thorough examination of your tank another time.' He patted Brock on the shoulder. Then he vaulted the fence and disappeared round the corner of the house.

Three

It was dinner time and Churchill Street was quiet and deserted. Brock's Dad sat bolt upright as he rode slowly along the street, staring straight in front of him, as his legs moved round in slow motion. His face showed absolute concentration on what he was doing. Yet he must have caught a glimpse of Whitman, because as he pushed his own heavy bike through the gate, he asked suspiciously:

'What was that boy after?'

'He only came to see my bike,' Brock told him, trying to appear innocent.

'Well, don't let me catch you giving him a ride,' he said, as he reached down for his trouser clips. He opened the wash-house door and wheeled his bike inside. When he came out he looked at Brock's bike.

'Well, are you pleased?' he asked.

'Yes, thank you,' Brock lied.

'That's the idea,' Dad said. 'I knew you would be when you saw it.' Then, taking off his cap, he went into the house.

It had been a dreadful morning, but Brock wasn't feeling too bad. There was still his birthday party to look forward to. All Brock's friends had been invited, all of them that is except Whitman. Brock tried to explain to Mum. Whitman, was one of the gang, and he did live next door. But it didn't make any difference with Brock's Mum.

'I'm not making tea for that boy,' she said emphatically. 'In any case he's too old to come to your party. And Dad thinks the same too.' Last year Whitman had been cheeky to Dad about the way Dad rode his bike, and Mum and Dad had never forgotten it. Since then Whitman had not been allowed inside their house.

Brock only had a small dinner, because he still had his chocolates to eat, and because tea for the gang was at four o'clock. Brock was determined to eat more than anybody else if it was the last thing he did. After all it was his party. Dad was reading a book and Mum was washing the dishes, so Brock went outside again. He was pumping up the tyres on his bike when Fagin arrived.

Fagin was Brock's best friend. He was only three months older than Brock and they went to the same school together. Fagin was almost as small as Brock and he was quiet and shy. He hardly ever spoke unless somebody spoke to him first. But he wasn't frightened of anybody. Even Whitman wouldn't have dared to start a fight with him.

Fagin's real name was Franklin Jones, but he didn't like his name, so all his friends called him Fagin.

'This is my birthday bike,' Brock explained, offering Fagin a chocolate. Fagin took the strawberry cream. Brock had wanted that one himself.

Fagin stood next to Brock, gazing at the bike without saying a word. Brock wished he'd have said something for then he would have known what Fagin was thinking.

They ate all the chocolates between them, and Brock had just put the box in the dustbin when the rest of the gang arrived. The rest of the gang were Alan Scott, nicknamed Scotty, and Raymond Clayton. Scotty was tall and thin, so thin he had to have his clothes specially made for him. Clayton was Scotty's shadow. He followed Scotty everywhere. And anything Scotty did, Clayton wanted to do with him.

Fagin, Scotty and Clayton crowded round Brock's bike.

'What's this, Titch?' Clayton asked.

'My mum and dad gave it me for my birthday,' Brock told them.

'When was it built?' Scotty inquired.

'It was made by the Army.'

'They didn't win the war with it?' Clayton cackled. He winked at Scotty and they both broke into fits of laughter.

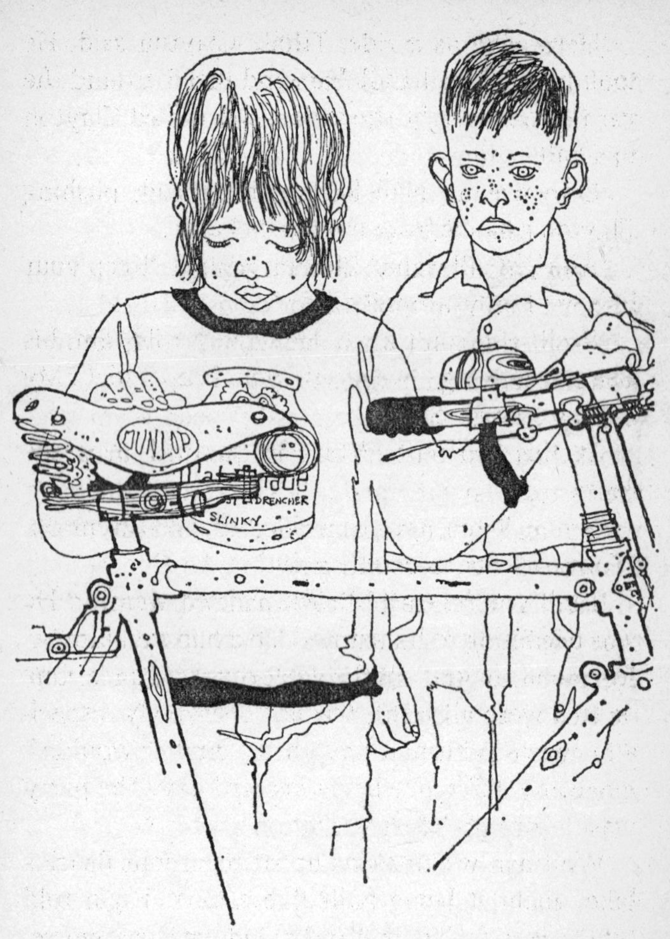

'What do you do with it – sit up and beg!' Scotty spluttered.

Brock pursed his lips. It was exactly the same as with Whitman. They were making jokes about his bike.

'Here, give us a ride, Titch,' Clayton said. He took hold of the handlebars and raced around the yard. Brock caught the saddle and pulled Clayton to a halt.

'Give me my bike back,' Brock said, pushing Clayton's hands from the handlebars.

'All right, all right,' Clayton replied. 'Keep your hair on. I only wanted a ride.'

'Well, you can't have one,' Brock told him, his voice trembling. 'And will you keep quiet. My dad's reading a book.'

At this moment Whitman jumped over the fence.

'Go on, Titch, give us a ride,' Clayton went on. 'Your dad'll be asleep by now.'

'I tell you he isn't,' Brock insisted wearily. He was beginning to be worried. Dad had told him before about having all the gang round at once. One or two were all right, but not everybody, especially when Whitman was there. And it wouldn't make any difference being his birthday. The party wasn't for two hours yet.

Whitman was making up stories about Brock's bike, about it being built like a tank. Fagin told him to stop it, but that only made matters worse. Whitman climbed astride the gate and swung it backwards and forwards against the trellis fence. Altogether they were making a tremendous row. Something was bound to happen and sure enough it did. Suddenly there was violent banging on the landing window. Scotty gave a nervous squeak and jumped off the ground with fright. In the fraction of a second the yard went silent. Nobody looked up at the window, but they all knew Brock's Dad was standing there. Dad hammered on the glass a second time. Brock held his breath and waited.

'Take those boys away from here,' Dad shouted.

When Whitman went on swinging on the gate, Dad fumbled with the window catch. He opened it with a clatter. There was a ferocious expression on his face.

'John,' he bellowed. 'Tell that boy he'll pay for our gate if it comes off its hinges.' Whitman jumped down, shook his head, and held out his hands in from of him. Clayton wheeled Brock's bike onto the road and propped it against the curb.

'Let's go to my house,' he said, putting his tongue out at the window after Brock's Dad had disappeared. 'I'm not staying here with the Great Dictator in a temper like this.'

'I'm not coming,' Whitman told them. 'I've arranged to see a client about my new bike. I'll let you know what transpires later on.' He pretended to chop off a rose in Brock's garden with the back of his hand. Scotty and Clayton raised clenched fists in the air, which was the gang's secret sign. Whitman did it back to them.

Then he got his new bike out of his wash-house and carried it with one finger onto the road. The last they saw of him was the bike swerving at an angle of forty-five degrees as Whitman went round the corner at the bottom of the street. His legs moved round and round in powerful circular motions. He must have been travelling at least twenty-five miles an hour.

'What a bike,' Clayton said.

'Wish I had it,' Scotty added.

'Give you a race to that car,' Clayton called out. He had a start, but Scotty still beat him.

Brock checked the gate was latched properly. He thought of leaving the bike behind, but if he had, Clayton would have nagged and nagged about his ride. Fagin was waiting for him by the lamppost on the green. Scotty and Clayton crossed the main road into the old part of the village. Fagin and Brock hurried after them.

They went over the level-crossing, turned into Fern Avenue, and met Clayton's Mum with a bagful of shopping.

'Hello, darling,' she called, waving her white-gloved hand to Clayton. Clayton ran up to her and took a banana, which was sticking out of the shopping bag.

'I'm making a cup of tea,' Clayton's Mum told them, as she went into the house.

'We'll have orange juice,' Clayton gabbled. His mouth was stuffed full of banana.

The others waited in the drive while Clayton

went for the bat and ball. They always played cricket at Clayton's house because the driveway was long and Clayton had three wickets painted on his garage doors.

'My first innings,' Clayton said, coming out through the front door. Scotty took the ball and marked out his run. With his second delivery Clayton was L.B.W.

'My go,' Fagin said. Clayton shuffled his front foot.

'I wasn't out,' Clayton argued. 'Look at my leg.'

'Come on, Raymond,' Scotty said.

'No – I'm not out,' Clayton shouted.

'Play the game,' Brock told him. Fagin walked up to Clayton and took the bat out of his hands. Clayton tried to get it back, but Fagin pushed him away. Immediately Clayton went to Scotty.

'I'd like my ball, Alan.'

'You were out Raymond.'

'My ball please,' Clayton went on. Scotty dropped it on the ground and Clayton caught it on the bounce.

'He's a great baby,' Brock said to Fagin. Clayton rushed to Brock, caught hold of his jumper and thrust his nose into Brock's face.

'Say that again,' Clayton taunted Brock. Brock backed away.

'Go on, say it. Say it again.'

'Leave Brock alone,' Fagin told Clayton.

'Stay out of this, Jones,' Clayton screeched. 'Mind you own business.' Clayton shoved Brock against the garage doors with his shoulders.

'Are you there, Raymond?' Clayton's Mum called.

'We'll be in in a minute,' Clayton said. 'I just want a ride on John's new bike.'

'Isn't it your birthday, John?' Clayton's Mum asked.

'Yes,' Brock answered. 'I'm eleven years old today.'

Clayton wobbled round the driveway and fell into a clump of undergrowth.

'Do be careful, Raymond,' Clayton's Mum said.

'I'm glad it isn't mine,' Clayton retorted. 'It would be safer driving a tank.'

Brock pulled the bike upright.

'I can't stay any longer,' Fagin said suddenly.

'Oh, what a pity,' Clayton's Mum replied.

'I'd better go as well,' Brock told her. 'My mum wants me to help her with my party.'

Brock climbed onto his bike. Clayton's Mum stood in the doorway.

'Good-bye,' she said. 'I hope you have a nice party.'

Fagin held onto the saddle and Brock pulled him along. The gates were closed at the level-crossing. While they were waiting for the train Fagin let

Brock punch him in the stomach. Fagin was Brock's bodyguard. Brock hit him as hard as he could but Fagin didn't even flinch. His muscles were like steel.

Past the shops they saw Brian Anderson, running along on the other side of the road. Brock guessed he must have been to see Whitman about the new racing-bike.

I wonder if he's bought it, Brock thought.

Brian Anderson didn't see them and Brock was glad, because he was beginning to feel ashamed of his tank. Since Whitman had called it that name Brock couldn't think of his bike as anything else.

Mum must have seen them coming, because she came out to meet them.

'I'm glad I've found you,' she said. 'I haven't had a chance to make a single sandwich yet.'

'I'll help,' Brock told her.

'See you later, Brock,' Fagin called, as he walked off down the street.

'What a pleasant boy that Franklin Jones is,' she said. Brock put 'The Tank' in the wash-house and then followed Mum into the kitchen.

'If you'll start by laying the table in the front room?' Mum asked him. She was icing his birthday cake. While Brock laid out the tray, Mum gave him a long lecture about the gang making so much noise.

'You know how it upsets Dad,' she said. 'And he does like to be quiet after his Saturday dinner.'

'Sorry,' Brock answered glumly.

'Never mind, dear,' Mum said. 'Let's forget all about it. The last thing I want is to spoil your birthday. Anyway you're not the only one who's in trouble. That boy, David Whitman, has been in a real row with his father.'

'What happened?' Brock asked. He liked to hear about other people's rows, especially when Whitman was involved.

'Well, that boy, David Whitman, had his friend in the house. You know his name.'

'Brian Anderson.'

'That's it, Brian Anderson. They had such a quarrel between the pair of them. I've never heard anything like it. Mr Whitman was in the garden, but he must have heard it from there. He told them to stop immediately, but that boy wouldn't listen and he was cheeky and he tried to argue. In the end Mr Whitman lost his temper, which is most unusual for him, though I'm not surprised. If you were the same I don't know what your father would say.'

Brock picked up the tray and carried it into the front room.

It was always the same with Whitman, he thought. He was all right with the gang because they were younger than he was, but as soon as Whitman tried to be friends with somebody his own age, things went wrong. Whitman liked to be boss and have other people look up to him.

After laying the table, Brock buttered the bread and opened two tins of salmon.

'What shall I do now?' Brock asked. Mum was slicing a chocolate roll. She seemed to be measuring the slices and thinking at the same time.

'I know,' she said after several seconds. 'You can lay out the Monopoly board on the coffee table. Your friends always play when they come here.'

Brock was doing that, when there was a knock at the front door.

'Will you please answer it?' Mum called. As Brock reached the hallway the knocking came again, only louder. He wondered who it could be. The party wasn't due to start for another half hour. When Brock opened the door, he found Whitman in front of him with tears in his eyes. It was the first time Brock had ever seen Whitman crying. Whitman stood there not saying anything. Brock couldn't think what to do. Then Whitman pulled a brown paper parcel from under his jumper and thrust it into Brock's hands.

'This is for you,' he sniffed. 'It's for your birthday. And I want you and the gang to come with me to the Tilburn Hills tomorrow.'

Then he was gone, before Brock had a chance to thank him.

'Who was it?' Mum asked curiously.

'It was David Whitman,' Brock told her. 'He's brought me a birthday present.' Mum didn't say anything about the parcel, not even that it was nice of Whitman to have thought of his birthday.

'I must go and change,' Mum said. 'Your friends will be here in a minute.'

Brock found a pair of scissors in the cabinet drawer. He cut the string and pulled away the brown paper wrapping. Inside was a silver bicycle bell. Brock was really pleased. He took the bell upstairs and showed it to Mum.

'Isn't it good?' he said.

'Very nice,' she answered, but she didn't look at the bell.

'I'll have to invite him to the party now,' Brock told her, picking up a hairbrush from the dressing-table. Mum looked at her face in the mirror.

'I can't do anything else, not after he's given me this bell.'

'I'm not at all sure, John.'

'Oh! Please, Mum.'

'We ought to see what Dad thinks.'

'Where is he?' Brock demanded impatiently.

'He's gone to the library. You'll have to wait till he comes back.'

'It'll be too late then,' Brock told her. 'Dad's always hours at the library.'

Mum didn't say anything to this.

'Go on, Mum,' Brock begged.

'No. I'm sorry, John,' she said. 'I said no and I meant no.' Brock clucked his tongue and gave a knowing grunt.

'And you needn't make those noises,' she told him. 'Now I'd like you to tidy your bedroom in case any of your friends go up there.'

It was Brock's turn not to answer. He ran his thumb backwards and forwards through the bristles of the hairbrush.

'John, I just spoke to you.'

'Pardon?'

'I want you to tidy your bedroom,' Mum said loudly with slow deliberation. 'And will you stop playing with my hairbrush.'

'All right,' Brock answered sulkily.

He just couldn't be bothered to tidy his bedroom. Not that there was anything wrong with it. He straightened the pillow and pulled the counterpane over the top of it. Then he took down his piggy-bank from the window ledge and emptied the money onto the dressing-table. The postal orders were there too. Mum must have put them in the piggy-bank this morning. Eight pounds and fifteen pence altogether. And it was no use to him. He still didn't have a racing-bike. He had thought this was to be his happiest birthday, and instead his friends had made jokes about him. The gang had always laughed at him, because he was the youngest and because he was so small. And 'The Tank' only made matters worse. With a racing-bike it might have been different. But that wasn't to be after all.

Four

Scotty didn't have a Mum. She died when Scotty was three years old. He had a housekeeper now, called Miss Stable, who did the cooking for Scotty and his Dad. And she was terribly strict with Scotty. He had to do exactly what she said.

Scotty was very clever and last year he came top of his class. His bedroom was full of books. If the gang wanted to know anything – anything whatsoever – they asked Scotty. Yet despite his cleverness Scotty was very nervous, and sometimes he wasn't even able to speak without stuttering.

Brock saw Scotty cross the green from his bedroom window. He needed only a glance at the flat parcel under Scotty's long thin arm to know that one of his presents would be a very difficult book. As Brock undid the parcel, he hoped it might be an adventure story, but it wasn't. Scotty had bought him 'History of Everyday Things in Medieval England'.

'I think you'll like it,' Scotty said.

'You'll learn a lot from that book,' Mum told Brock cheerfully.

'Let me read you the beginning,' Scotty said. He took the book from Brock and opened it at the front.

'Sit down and listen to Alan,' Mum said.

Scotty had just started reading when there was another knock at the door.

'I'll answer it,' Mum called from the kitchen. A few moments later Clayton appeared in the doorway. He was grinning all over his face. In his arms was a red box-shaped parcel, which was almost too large for him to carry. Clayton was wearing his best blue suit, with a white shirt and silk bow-tie. His round cheeks shone and there wasn't a strand of his sleek black hair out of place.

'Oh, hello, Mrs Brockson,' he said; then he smiled sweetly. 'And this is for you, John,' Clayton added, turning to Brock. 'I hope you have a happy birthday.'

Brock took the parcel and tore off the bright red paper which covered it. Underneath was a cardboard box. The lid was held down by strips of Sellotape. Inside there were screwed-up balls of newspaper. Brock pulled out twelve of them. At the very bottom of the box was a pair of blue jeans. Brock could hardly believe his eyes. Clayton's Mum always bought the best presents, but he hadn't expected anything as good as this.

'Look at them, Mum,' Brock shouted. Mum came through from the kitchen.

'Just what I wanted,' he told her. 'I'm going to try them on.' Mum had a blank expression on her face as Brock went past her up the stairs. She wasn't very pleased and he thought he knew why. After this she wouldn't be able to buy him any more short trousers.

Brock tried them on in his bedroom.

My first long trousers, he thought proudly. It was like wearing pyjamas. They went right down to his shoes and they fitted perfectly.

'Good old Clayton,' he said to himself. He ran into Mum's bedroom and looked at himself in the tall mirror. For a moment he hardly recognized himself. He seemed to have grown into a giant. None of the gang could call him Titch now.

There was another knock at the door, but he let somebody else answer it. He turned the mirror so he could see the back of himself in the dressing-table mirror. Brock wiggled his hips and jumped in the air. He was just like a cowboy in a Western film. He swaggered downstairs into the dining-room and pulled imaginary guns on everybody.

Fagin had arrived. He was standing on his own by the mantelpiece. When he saw Brock's jeans he turned away and placed a small box on the shelf. Scotty and Clayton were sitting by the coffee table. They had the Monopoly money divided into four piles.

‘Ready,’ Clayton called out. Scotty was shaking the dice in the egg-cup when Mum came in and interrupted them.

‘John dear,’ she said, Franklin has brought you a present. I think the very least you can do is to open it.’

‘It doesn’t matter,’ Fagin mumbled, turning away with embarrassment.

‘Let’s have the game of Monopoly first,’ Clayton said, but it was too late. Mum had already taken the box down from the mantelshelf. Brock had to open it. Inside were two white handkerchiefs.

‘Thank you very much,’ Brock said.

Fagin didn’t answer. He pretended to be arranging his money. Brock could tell Fagin was upset. He understood how he felt, especially after Clayton had given him the jeans. And Fagin was Brock’s best friend. Brock wouldn’t have opened the box till everybody had gone home, though Mum wasn’t to have known. Still, he couldn’t help being annoyed.

‘We want tea,’ he demanded loudly, banging the coffee table with his fist. Mum gave Brock a hard disapproving stare and then walked out of the room.

Fagin was even quieter than usual, though he got over the upset when he started to win the game of Monopoly. At first Scotty accumulated large sums of money, and he tried to make everybody bankrupt. But then Fagin threw two double-sixes.

Scotty said Fagin had been holding the egg-cup incorrectly, but it was no use. In the end he had to hand over nearly a thousand pounds. Five minutes later Fagin had won.

'Well played,' Brock told Fagin.

'It was only a fluke, Alan,' Clayton said.

'Not at all,' Brock argued. 'It was mind against matter.'

'Shut up, Brockson. You fat little cheat,' Clayton shouted.

'Yellow belly,' Brock answered back. Clayton threatened to start a fight but he didn't dare, not while they were in Brock's house. Anyway Fagin would have stuck up for Brock. Scotty said the only fair solution was to have another game. They agreed to do that, and Scotty was dividing the money again, when Mum came in and said she had everything ready.

'I called you four times,' she told them. 'Didn't any of you hear?'

Tea was laid out on the table in the living-room. There was a paper hat in everybody's place and Mum had printed their names on cards, which were attached to the chairs. Brock was sitting next to Fagin, and Scotty and Clayton were together. Mum handed round the tomato sandwiches and everybody took one politely. But as soon as Mum left the room Clayton snatched three chocolate rolls and finished off the jug of lemonade.

He would have had twice as much as Brock if Mum hadn't come in with the matches for lighting the candles. Clayton wiped chocolate cream from his mouth and offered a plate of sausages on sticks to Fagin. Fagin shook his head. He couldn't speak because his mouth was full of potato crisps. He'd eaten the whole bowlful himself. There were only a few crumbs remaining at the bottom of the bowl. Mum gave Brock the matches and he lit the eleven candles. He felt the warmth of the flame on his face. Coloured wax ran down the candles onto the white icing. It reminded him of last Christmas, when there had been snow outside.

'Happy birthday,' Mum sang. 'Happy birthday to you.' And they all joined in. Brock wanted to join in too, but he remembered just in time that he wasn't supposed to. He sat and listened to the singing, which was just for him, though he didn't enjoy it because he was too embarrassed. Half way through the song, Mum told them she'd a kettle boiling. The moment she left Clayton changed to a different rhyme about squashed tomatoes and stew. He stood on his chair and threw his arms about wildly, singing and conducting at the same time. They were all singing at the tops of their voices, completely involved in the movements of Clayton's hands.

Brock saw Dad first. As he passed the window he must have seen Clayton, because he got off his bike and wheeled it onto the pavement. He stood there staring at them until Scotty coughed, which was the gang's sign for 'danger'. Clayton stopped conducting, his arms suspended in the air. His face turned red as he sat down. Brock blew out all the candles first time and they pretended to watch the wisps of smoke rising from the cake.

Nobody said a word. Brock pulled out the candles, and divided the cake into six, one piece for each of them, and a piece for Mum and Dad. Everybody took one. They all looked sheepish as Dad opened the door.

'Hello,' he said. 'Are you enjoying yourselves?'

Fagin, Scotty and Clayton muttered something which sounded like 'Thank you'. Dad reached down for his bicycle-clips, half-smiled and then disappeared into the kitchen. As soon as Scotty had finished his cake, he took off his hat and wiped his hands on it.

'I – think – I'd – better be going home,' he said nervously.

'Let's all go to my house,' Clayton suggested.

They were about to do this when Mum came in.

'I've some news for you,' she told Brock. 'Dad has met an old friend at the library and he's invited Dad and me to his house. We shouldn't be away more than a couple of hours.' She paused and then added, 'You don't mind us leaving you like this on your birthday?'

'No – no, not at all,' Brock answered. It was almost too good to be true. The gang were to have the house all to themselves.

Five minutes later, Mum called out: 'That's me, Frank.' Dad held the door for her.

'Be sure to keep the pantry closed,' Mum reminded Brock. 'And watch out for Mollie. She's gone off somewhere. I've left the kitchen door open but she's probably frightened with all these people in the house.'

The gang stood at the window and watched Mum and Dad walk down the street. As soon as they'd disappeared from view, Clayton switched on the television. It boomed on at full volume, and then the picture came into focus. A western film was just starting. Fagin, Scotty and Clayton crowded round the set. Brock carefully lifted the crease in his long trousers and sat down beside them. Four horsemen were riding over a hill. A tribe of Indians were waiting for them. The leader raised his tomahawk in the air and let out a piercing war cry.

Five

Whitman swung round the corner at the bottom of Churchill Street. A girl came after him on another bike, but she wasn't fast enough to keep up.

'Here's Whitman and Judith,' Scotty shouted.

They all rushed to the window. Sunlight reflected on revolving spokes. Whitman's bike was made up of a number of lines and curves, which complemented each other perfectly. Brock had never seen anything so beautiful.

Whitman came along as fast as a car, and when he was opposite Brock's house he pulled on the brakes. The bike stopped dead. Whitman propped it against the pavement by its pedal. Clayton gave the hand on head sign for 'All clear'. Whitman jumped over the low wall and banged on the window. Clayton opened it for him and Whitman climbed in. By this time his girlfriend had arrived at the front door. Whitman opened it for her and they came into the room.

'Did you sell the bike?' Clayton asked.

'No such luck,' Whitman answered. 'But plenty

of time. Any number of people will give their right arm for a bike like mine. It's only a question of waiting and choosing the suitable client.'

Everybody except Brock laughed.

'Well, where's my slice of birthday cake?' Whitman asked.

'It's all gone,' Brock told him.

'There's gratitude for you,' Whitman smirked.

'Titch has new trousers,' Clayton said.

'So I observe,' Whitman replied, feeling the material between his fingers. 'Quite the young gentleman about town. And somebody sent you a picture of your Tank, I see.' He went over to the mantelpiece and picked up the card of the penny-farthing. Everybody was laughing again.

'Leave my Johnny alone,' Judith said, sitting next to Brock on the sofa. Clayton whistled and jeered, 'Give us a kiss, Titch.'

Brock felt himself blushing.

He couldn't imagine why Judith went out with Whitman. She was such a pretty girl in her sailor-suit and with her long black hair. Perhaps Judith was in love with *him* and she went with Whitman just so as to be able to see Brock now and then.

'Move over, Titch,' Whitman said, pushing Brock off the sofa. He sat down himself, and then started talking about their trip to the Tilburn Hills.

'I'd like to make an early start about nine,' he explained. 'Before any of the Sunday traffic gets on the road. It's only fifteen miles so there shouldn't be any difficulties. The last two hills are quite steep and Titch will probably need to get off his Tank and push. But coming back it's freewheeling all the way, so I expect to be home by three.'

Meanwhile Clayton had opened Dad's bureau.

'What do you think you're doing?' Brock asked him.

'Searching for love letters,' Clayton answered nonchalantly. 'I found some of my dad's. They were hidden in his desk.'

'You've to stop at once,' Brock gasped. His mouth was dry and he felt an uncontrollable panic coming over him. 'My dad knows the exact position of every paper and document. He can tell immediately if anything's been touched. Even my mum isn't allowed in there.'

'Not to worry, Titch,' Clayton said. He pulled out the top drawer and began sorting through the papers.

Brock went over to the window and looked out. Mrs Fox in the house opposite was watching them. If she saw what was going on she'd be bound to tell Mum. Brock stepped back and drew the curtains. He was terrified. What if Mum and Dad came home early! Dad would be furious with him for having Whitman in the house, and the bureau would make matters ten times worse. That was the trouble with the gang. They didn't listen to a word he said. And it was his house. He was the one who got the blame, not them.

When the clock in the hall struck eight, Brock summoned up his courage. With thumping heart and hot face he said: 'David, please will you go?'

Whitman ignored him. He continued talking to Scotty about his bike.

'Of course I would be surprised if there's another one like it in the world. At thirty pounds I'm giving it away. The parts alone would cost you more than that in Percy's cycle shop.'

'Will you please leave,' Brock told him again.

Whitman paused, looked down into Brock's anxious face and said patiently,

'That's all right, Titch. You can leave everything to me. I'll take care of your dad.'

Brock was desperate. He couldn't think what to say. Fortunately Judith stood up and asked Whitman to take her home. Brock heaved a sigh of relief when Whitman agreed.

'I'll have to speak to your father another evening,' Whitman said, imitating Dad's manner of speaking through his false teeth.

But at that moment, Scotty who had been on guard at the window, gave the alarm. Brock's Mum and Dad had turned the corner at the bottom of the street.

'You can go through the kitchen,' Brock told Whitman.

Whitman didn't move a step.

'I'm not taking my girl through your back entrance,' he exclaimed indignantly. 'If your father wishes to speak to me, we'll stay right here until he arrives.'

Scotty gave a nervous giggle. Brock looked at Fagin sitting by himself close to the television set. He had been there since the Western had started.

'You must leave, Whitman,' he pleaded. 'I'll be in terrible trouble if you're found here.'

Whitman snorted. Very slowly he passed a hand through his curly red hair.

'Allow your Uncle David to take charge of the situation,' he said calmly, leaning with one hand against the mantelpiece. Brock shut his eyes. What was he to do? He tried to think. In a few seconds Dad would come through the door. He had to make a decision. Brock took hold of Whitman's jumper and tried to drag him towards the kitchen, but it was no use. Whitman was much too strong for him. Brock let go and ran out of the house to meet Mum and Dad. He had no idea what he could do, but if he wasn't there when Whitman was caught, he could at least say he had asked Whitman to leave.

It was a beautiful summer evening. The sun was low in the sky and long shadows were cast across the road from the houses on the other side of the street. Mum and Dad's footsteps echoed in the cool still air. Dad was pointing to some roses in one of the front gardens, and he was telling Mum about a visit he had to make to London. They ambled along arm in arm and they were so engrossed in their conversation that they didn't see the small figure of Brock outside the house. Brock gave a frightened groan.

'Oh, hello, John,' Mum called. 'Have you enjoyed yourselves?'

'Yes, thank you,' Brock replied, going to meet them. 'You seemed such a long time, I came out to see if you were coming.'

'We did rather stay talking,' Mum said.

Perhaps it won't be too bad, Brock thought. After all it is my birthday.

The curtains were tightly drawn as they walked up the path. Dad stared at the two bikes outside their house, but he didn't say anything. There wasn't a sound from the dining-room. Brock felt as though he was walking straight into a trap.

'I trust you've behaved yourselves,' Dad said, as he went through the front door.

Brock made certain he was last. He wanted to be near Mum when Dad and Whitman confronted one another.

Fagin, Scotty, Clayton and Judith were playing Monopoly on the coffee table. Scotty had just thrown a double-six and won one hundred pounds. Clayton glanced up and politely said,

'Good evening, Mr and Mrs Brockson.'

Neither Mum nor Dad answered him.

'Your go again,' Judith said, handing Scotty the egg-cup.

Brock edged towards the sofa and leaned over

it. Whitman wasn't there. Dad stood in the doorway and surveyed the room. He was obviously suspicious, firstly because Judith was in the house, secondly because of the two bikes outside, and lastly because he had an instinct for things when they were wrong.

'Why are those curtains drawn?' he demanded.

'It was starting to get dark,' Clayton answered, almost before Dad had finished speaking.

Dad grunted, drew back the curtains and looked out at the two bikes.

'I think I'll make a cup of tea,' he said to Mum.

'That would be lovely, Frank,' she told him.

Dad walked into the kitchen, his eyes darting about in every direction.

Brock couldn't see any clues which might give them away. But where was Whitman? Brock expected him to be caught at any moment. He had a horrible vision of Dad dragging Whitman out of the house by his curly red hair.

It was abnormally quiet. The only sound was the dice being thrown on the board.

'Go back three paces,' Fagin said to Scotty.

Brock noticed that Scotty's hand was trembling, as he moved the battleship across the board. Dad came back into the room and stared at the bureau. It was as if a secret agent had explained to him about Clayton having the papers out. Brock wondered if Clayton had replaced them in the correct order.

'And how is David?' Dad asked Judith.

'Oh, he's quite well, thank you,' Judith answered softly. She was acting as if everything was perfectly normal.

Mum took off her coat and dropped it over the sofa.

'Has there been any sign of Mollie?' she inquired.

'No – no, we haven't seen her,' Brock told her hurriedly, twining his fingers together. He didn't seem to be able to keep his hands still. Dad coughed. As he did so there was a loud thud from above. Brock stared at the carpet and waited.

Dad frowned, cocked his head on one side and listened.

When nothing further happened, he opened the door and started up the stairs. He had gone three steps when there was a heavy thump outside. A second later the figure of Whitman crossed the front window. And then Brock understood how Whitman had made his escape. He must have hidden upstairs, and then climbed out of Brock's bedroom window onto the porch by the front door. Once on the porch, it was a simple matter to jump down onto the lawn.

'Did you hear that noise?' Dad asked, coming

back into the room. There was a puzzled expression on his face.

'It must have been Mollie,' Mum told him.

Dad stared at them all in disbelief.

'I think the kettle's boiling,' Mum added.

Dad frowned and then disappeared into the kitchen.

By this time Judith had packed the Monopoly set back in its box. The gang stood up.

Judith opened the door.

'Thank you for a lovely party, Mrs Brockson,' Clayton said. The others thanked Mum too.

'I'm walking to the corner with Franklin,' Brock told Mum.

When he came back the bikes had gone from outside the house. Whitman and Judith were nowhere in sight. Mum winked at Brock as he crept through the kitchen. She whispered, 'Dad is reading a book,' which meant it was best not to disturb him.

Brock picked up Fagin's handkerchiefs and Scotty's book and then slunk upstairs to his bedroom. He went to the window and peered down on to the porch.

What a stroke of luck for Whitman, he thought, smiling to himself as he undressed. He lay in bed, and after Mum had said good night to him, he thought of his new bike and how very different it was from Whitman's bike. Dad would have bought him a racing-bike if he'd really understood how Brock felt, but he didn't understand: Brock knew he didn't, and there didn't seem anything could change that.

Six

It had been raining outside. Brock could tell by the heavy dampness in the air. He climbed out of bed and drew back the curtains. Droplets of rain were spattered against the window pane, and patches of wetness clung to the pavements. Heavy dark clouds scudded low across a grey sky. Brock shivered in his pyjamas. It was cold for July.

Not the day for a long ride, he thought. But it was all arranged and Brock wouldn't be the first to back out. He could hear Mum cooking Dad's breakfast downstairs. And there was the smell of frying eggs and bacon. Dad had breakfast in bed every Sunday morning. Afterwards he went to sleep again. Brock would need to hurry or he'd have the gang outside the house. The last thing he wanted was another row with Dad. Brock dressed quickly. He put on his birthday blue jeans, and his thick blue jumper to go with it. It reminded him of feeling like a cowboy. 'The Tank' would be his faithful horse.

Downstairs, Mum was laying the breakfast tray

for two. She was still in her night-gown and slippers.

'Hello, John,' she said with a tired smile. 'You're up early this morning.'

Brock explained to her about going to the Tilburn Hills. He half-expected her to object and she did.

'It's not the sort of weather for cycling,' she said.

'I'll shelter if it rains again,' he promised.

'Wouldn't it be better if you went by bus?'

'There aren't any buses to the Tilburn Hills on a Sunday.'

Mum thought for a few seconds.

'It's an awful distance,' she said. 'I'd better make you some sandwiches.'

'There isn't time,' Brock told her. 'I'm late as it is.'

In the end Mum agreed, but she made him take Dad's plastic mac and tie it to the back of the saddle.

'And be careful you don't tear it,' she warned.

'Don't worry,' Brock told her. 'I'll look after it.' He gulped down a glass of milk and ate two rounds of toast.

As he wheeled 'The Tank' through the gate Mum called softly from the front window.

'When will you be home?'

'Three o'clock.'

'Take this,' she hissed, holding out a ten pence piece. 'You're sure to feel hungry.'

Brock propped 'The Tank' on the pavement, ran back to the open window and took the money from her outstretched hand. She patted him on the head, nodded and then shut the window.

Brock scrambled onto 'The Tank' and pedalled furiously towards the other end of the village. The gang had all agreed to meet at Clayton's house. It was abnormally quiet at this time of the morning. Curtains were drawn in most of the windows, and cars stood in driveways, their windscreens filmed with dew. Brock hesitated at the T-junction. There was nothing coming on the main road. He crossed, and rode on even faster. A horrible acid taste rose into his mouth, a mixture of milk, marmalade, butter and toast. No matter how many times he swallowed, it would not go away.

When Brock turned into Fern Avenue the gang was waiting outside Clayton's house.

'You're late,' Clayton shouted, and before he could catch up, Scotty and Clayton rode on ahead. But Fagin waited for him. As usual he was wearing his grey jumper and long grey trousers.

'They wanted to go without you,' he told Brock. 'But I threatened to let down their tyres if they tried.'

'What about Whitman?' Brock asked.

'He's gone to fetch Judith,' Fagin explained. 'They're coming on later.'

Together they raced after the disappearing figures of Scotty and Clayton. It took them a long time to catch up, and Fagin didn't find it any easier than Brock, because his bike was as small as Brock's was large. He'd had that same bike since he was seven, and both Fagin and Brock had learnt to ride on it.

Once out of the village the roads became narrow and winding. The countryside was deserted and peaceful. There were only them, the green fields, the cows, the sheep, and the birds which flitted between the humming telegraph wires. And occasionally they passed a farmer on a tractor.

What it is to have a bike, Brock thought. I've never been here before, and without my bike I wouldn't have been able to.

There was a strong breeze, but it was behind them. Brock was beginning to think 'The Tank' wasn't so bad after all. Most of the time he kept up without any difficulty, though going up the hills wasn't quite so easy. Scotty and Clayton would disappear from sight ahead of them. Then without saying a word Fagin pedalled faster. He did it without any effort and he didn't seem to notice Brock puffing and panting behind him. Still Brock managed to keep up. That was all he really cared about.

After an hour they came to a café by the side of the road. Scotty's and Clayton's bikes were propped outside. They both had the same make of bike though Clayton's was a wreck compared with Scotty's.

Fagin and Brock leaned their bikes against the café wall and went inside. Not until that moment did Brock realize how tiring a bike could be. As he eased himself into a chair it felt as if every bone in his body had been broken.

'You're like an old man,' Clayton told him.

'It's that Tank of his,' Scotty added.

'Everybody look out for a gravestone not in use,' Clayton spluttered. Both of them burst into fits of laughter. Clayton clutched his stomach and held onto the edge of the table.

'Don't take any notice,' Fagin told Brock. 'They're a couple of born idiots.'

'Listen who's talking,' Scotty retorted. He took out a map from his anorak, unfolded it on the table, and began to explain the way to Tilburn Hills.

They waited a long time and nobody came to serve them. There was a bell by the door, but it didn't seem to work. Clayton thumped on the table and shouted,

'Anybody at home!'

A huge Alsatian dog appeared from nowhere and began barking at them. They were ready to run when a fat grey-haired man appeared and quietened the dog down.

'All right – all right, Rex,' the man said reassuringly.

Rex sat down beside Fagin and Fagin patted him on the head.

The man was really friendly, wanted to know where they had come from and where they were going. Then he brought them a pot of tea and a plateful of scones.

Brock would gladly have sat in the café for the rest of the day, but a few minutes later Whitman and Judith came along on their bikes.

Whitman marched into the café as though he owned the place. He was wearing his white tracksuit with the cycling-club badge on the jacket. His long peaked cap was pulled down over his eyes. Judith was dressed all in white too. Together they were like two world champions.

'Come on you four,' he commanded, tipping Clayton off his chair.

'There's no hurry, David,' Judith said, but Whitman wouldn't listen to her.

The old man came rushing in to see what the commotion was.

'I thought something was wrong,' he told them. 'It's a good job I locked Rex in the garage.'

Clayton took a fifty pence piece out of his pocket and gave it to the man.

'There's two pence change,' he said.

'You can keep it,' Clayton told him grandly.

In less than a minute they were on their bikes again. Whitman raised a hand in the air, and raced ahead of them up the next hill.

'Wait for us,' Judith shouted.

When he didn't answer she went after him. Her bike was almost as good as Whitman's. He'd built it for her. They were both white. The only sound they made was the friction of the tyres on the road, and the tick of the cogs on the back wheels.

For a quarter of an hour or so Brock enjoyed the ride. Scotty and Clayton were trying to push each other off their bikes and they didn't go too fast. The tea and scones gave Brock a comfortable satisfied feeling in his stomach. For a short while he wasn't in the least tired. But then the hills became steeper. In no time at all Scotty and Clayton were dots in the distance. Fagin pedalled faster and Brock struggled after him.

Then suddenly the breeze changed to a strong wind, and with the wind came a fine misty rain. Brock could hardly feel it except for a warm clinging sensation around his face. Yet five minutes later his jumper and jeans were soaking. He knew he should have stopped, and put on Dad's plastic mac, but Fagin hadn't anything and he wasn't complaining. In any case they would have lagged even further behind. Brock was afraid they must have taken the wrong turning, because there was no sign of the others.

But at the bottom of the next hill they found Scotty and Clayton searching for berries in the hedgerows. They were both protected from the rain by their anoraks.

'I think I'll put my plastic mac on,' Brock said.

'I shouldn't bother,' Clayton told him. 'You look like a drowned rat already. Anyway it's only one more mile.'

If it had been any further Brock was certain he would have collapsed in the road. He was so cold, and there was a stabbing cramp in his legs. And when they did get there, the Tilburn Hills were hidden from view by the mist. There was only an old church, a row of houses and a bus shelter.

Whitman and Judith were inside the shelter.

'What have you been playing at?' Whitman called. 'We've been here nearly half an hour.'

Brock leaned 'The Tank' next to Whitman's bike. He had to look away.

Beside Whitman's bike, 'The Tank' was like something out of a museum.

'Watch my paintwork,' Whitman shouted at him.

Whitman had his arm round Judith's shoulder. He looked as fresh and as strong as he had done in the café, and that was seven miles away. They must have reached the Tilburn Hills before the mist came, because there wasn't a drop of moisture on either of them.

Whitman had a huge bar of chocolate in one hand. He was breaking pieces and feeding them into Judith's mouth. He was making her beg as if she was a performing seal.

All Brock wanted was dry warm clothes and then to lie down and sleep. He felt as though he could have slept for a week. The thought of having to cycle home filled him with dread. And the mist had changed to great gusts of rain, which were being swept in solid sheets across the moorside. Everywhere was wet. The tree trunks glistened black, thousands of droplets of water wobbled from the telegraph wires, the road streamed to overflowing. Even having to leave the bus shelter seemed too much of an ordeal to Brock. He closed his eyes and tried to relax, but Clayton wouldn't leave him alone.

'You should have seen Titch flashing past us,' Clayton was saying. 'We had to keep begging him to slow down.'

'It's this terrific Tank,' Scotty added. 'He's two cannons under the saddle and he fires them when he wants to accelerate.'

'That's right, isn't it, Titch?' Whitman shouted in Brock's ear.

Brock nodded his head wearily.

'Can't you see Brock's having a rest,' Fagin told them.

'Having a rest at his age?' Whitman chortled

'He ought to be running over that hill for the fun of it.'

'Don't listen to a word they say,' Judith said, with a kind smile.

Brock smiled weakly back at her.

Whitman stood up and lazily stretched his arms.

'Well, this rain's in for the day,' he said. 'No use hanging around here.' He took two yellow oilskins out of his saddlebag and gave one to Judith. She pulled it over her head, took out a tiny mirror, and began combing her hair.

Brock untied Dad's plastic mac and put it on. He had to roll the sleeves up, and the bottom almost touched the ground.

Of course Scotty and Clayton thought it was a great joke.

Brock took out the ten pence piece Mum had given him.

'I want to go to the next village for something to eat,' he informed them.

'There isn't time,' Whitman insisted. 'In any case they'll be shut by now. It's Sunday.'

'Anyway, that ten pence piece is mine,' Clayton said. 'You haven't paid for your share of the tea.'

Brock must have looked disheartened because Judith asked him if he was feeling well.

'It's my legs,' Brock complained, screwing up his face. 'I've got cramp in them.'

'David, you're to change bikes with Johnny,' Judith ordered.

'Ride "The Tank",' Whitman exploded. 'Never!'

'Go on,' Judith insisted. 'Do something nice for a change. Lend Johnny your bike.'

The amazing thing was – he did. Judith was the only person Whitman ever listened to. And she was a girl. Judith and Whitman were just like Mum and Dad in certain ways.

The rain drove into Brock's face, and the mist was all around them. Brock could scarcely see the others, though they were not far away. But riding Whitman's bike was like growing a pair of wings. There was something unnatural about it. Despite the howling wind, the bike seemed to speed forward on its own.

Brock felt as though it had been specially made for him. If only – Oh! – if only he could have had a bike like this.

'Do you see how he rides it?' Clayton called to Whitman.

Whitman didn't reply. He was straining at the pedals, attempting to keep up with the rest of the gang.

Brock could have ridden Whitman's bike all the way home, even though he wasn't able to sit on the saddle, and he was certain he wouldn't have had cramp again. Unfortunately Whitman refused to ride 'The Tank' any further after the first steep hill.

'You're best with this thing,' he told Brock insultingly, thrusting 'The Tank' into Brock's arms.

He took his own bike and rode on.

It was too good to last, Brock thought. At least I had a try on it.

Brock climbed on 'The Tank'. He struggled to catch up with Fagin.

After Whitman's bike 'The Tank' was a solid mass of cast iron. In no time at all the others were out of sight. Brock forced the pedals against the wind. There seemed to be nothing but the wind. It blew through the trees, tossing twigs into the road, and turning the leaves so their dull undersides were visible.

'Wait for me,' Brock shouted to Fagin, but the words were lost before they had left his mouth. The rain pelted into Brock's face, making him swing from one side of the road to the other. His forehead felt as if it had turned into ice.

A mile further on Whitman and the rest of the gang were waiting under a derelict barn.

'You'll need to do better than this,' Whitman said. 'We've decided to go to the pictures. If you can't cycle faster, we'll have to leave you behind.'

And that was the last they saw of Whitman and Judith. Scotty and Clayton stayed with them for a while, but then they too became tired of riding like snails. Fagin and Brock were left by themselves in the rain.

They had to stop every mile because of Brock's cramp. Fagin massaged his legs each time. But it got worse and worse and then he developed a sore on his bottom.

In the end Brock couldn't go on. Fagin found a telephone kiosk. He made Brock sit on the floor and do knee exercises, but it hardly made any difference.

'I wonder what time it is,' Brock said. His watch had stopped and Fagin didn't have one.

'I told my mum I'd be home for three. It must be nearly that now. If I'm more than half an hour late there's bound to be trouble.'

Brock thought of phoning Miss Stable and asking her to give Mum a message, but Clayton had taken Brock's ten pence piece, and Fagin didn't have any money either.

'Let's keep going,' Fagin said.

They started off once more. As they opened the kiosk door the rain burst in their faces. Brock hauled himself onto 'The Tank', forcing it into the wind.

They must have gone another mile when Brock's chain came off. Fagin came back to see what was wrong. He had the patience of a saint.

'Don't upset yourself,' he told Brock, freeing

the jammed chain from the frame. 'There can't be more than another five miles.'

'I can't go on,' Brock gasped. 'My hands have gone numb.'

'Just keep trying,' Fagin encouraged him.

Brock knew he had to find somewhere to rest.

Over another hill he saw a small cottage set back from the road.

'I'm stopping here,' Brock said.

'You don't know who lives there,' Fagin objected.

'I don't care,' Brock said. 'I'll ask if I can rest.'

He dropped his bike in the hedge and opened the gate. Fagin followed after him, but when he reached the front door, Fagin hid underneath an overhang.

There was a brass knocker in the shape of a gnome. Brock knocked three times, but nobody answered the door. He stood back and looked through a side window into the gloomy hallway. There didn't seem anybody about. But Brock wasn't giving up that easily. He knocked again and peered through the letterbox. As he did so he heard slow faltering footsteps.

A few seconds later the door creaked back and in the opening stood a stooped old, old woman. Brock was afraid of her, he was afraid of her shaking hands, her white hair and her dry wrinkled skin.

'What do you want?' she demanded suspiciously, peering into Brock's streaming wet face.

'I've lost my way,' Brock explained nervously. 'And I'm shivering with cold. Can I rest for five minutes – please?'

The old lady examined Brock's bedraggled form from head to foot. After hesitating a moment she nodded and then led him into a dark room, which faced on to a field of corn. It was warm and cosy inside the room and Brock stared in disbelief at the corn outside being dashed first one way, then another, by the raging wind. Rain battered against the window so hard that every so often the glass became clouded. The old lady went over to a black stove. She poured tea into a cup, then added milk and sugar.

'Drink this,' she told Brock. Brock held the steaming cup in both hands. The liquid went down his throat like fire. Water dripped from Dad's mac on to the stone floor. In no time at all a puddle had gathered beneath his feet.

Brock felt immeasurably better, though he'd only been out of the wind and rain for a few minutes. The hot drink had warmed his whole being.

'Thank you – thank you very much for letting me rest,' Brock said.

The old lady showed him to the door.

'I'm very grateful,' Brock shouted above the wind, and then he ran into the raging storm.

Fagin was standing where Brock had left him. He was very hurt when Brock told him he'd had a drink.

'What about me?' Fagin said angrily. 'You didn't think of me.'

'I'm sorry,' Brock told him. 'I really am sorry.' Fagin didn't say any more, but Brock knew he'd let his friend down. It was the first time they'd ever had a quarrel.

And it was all because of this stupid bike, Brock thought, as he climbed back on 'The Tank'. If I had a proper bike this would never have happened. Brock said he was sorry again.

'Forget it,' Fagin told him sympathetically. 'It's over and done with now.'

The rest of the journey wasn't nearly so bad. The road must have changed direction, because the wind was no longer against them. And the rain had slackened off too.

They had decided to have a bath and go to the pictures, but when they reached home Dad was really annoyed.

'Do you realize what time it is?' he shouted at Brock.

'My watch has stopped,' Brock explained.

'Well, it's half past five and your mother was expecting you home at three. We thought something had happened to you.'

Brock said it wasn't his fault, but that only upset Dad more.

'You can have a bath and go straight to bed,' Dad told him. 'And try and think of your mother another time.'

Brock showed Fagin to the door, put 'The Tank' in the wash-house, had his tea and then went upstairs to the bathroom.

Seven

It was still light when Brock climbed into bed. He allowed his body to sink into the soft shape of the mattress. It was wonderful just to be in dry clothes. Brock lay on his back. He hadn't the energy to move a muscle. His body felt as if every bone had changed position.

'What weather!' Mum said, when she came up to say good night. The wind was still howling outside.

'Well, I'm sure you're pleased with yourself,' Mum told him. 'Your first outing. Just think, you wouldn't have been able to do it without your new bike.'

It was later in bed that night Brock decided to save up and buy Whitman's bike. Why hadn't he thought of it before? It was the answer to all his problems, although he didn't exactly know how he would do it. But he already had eight pounds and fifteen pence. That left another twenty-one pounds and eighty-five pence to save. He couldn't prevent himself worrying in case somebody else bought Whitman's bike. Then what would he do? Yet he would save twenty-one pounds and eighty-five pence if it was the last thing he did.

He could just see himself beating Whitman in a long-distance race. Of course, it would be necessary to sell 'The Tank' but that ought not to be difficult. He'd put an advertisement in the window of the village grocery shop. Mum had done the same with her old washing-machine last year. It only cost ten pence for a whole week.

It took him ages to fall asleep. Thoughts of Whitman's bike plagued his mind. He couldn't think of anything else. Brock had never seen thirty pounds before. Thirty pounds was sixty weeks' pocket money. But he'd save thirty pounds. He would – he would – he would.

When he awoke his eyes were heavy and raw, and his body was stiff and unnatural, as if it didn't belong to him. Dad's alarm was ringing in the next bedroom, which meant it was nearly eight o'clock.

Brock looked at his watch. It showed half past three, but when he held it to his ear, Brock heard it was ticking again.

The wetness must have dried out, he thought.

Ten minutes later a chair scraped on the floor downstairs. Brock climbed out of bed and went over to the window. He was just in time to see Dad disappearing from view. Then he noticed that the wind had dropped. The pavements were dry and unusually white. Flowers in the gardens lay flat on the ground, as if somebody had pushed them over with a foot.

Brock turned back into the room and looked for his clothes. Mum had taken the jeans and his blue jumper, so he had to wear short trousers and a shirt. Normally it might have annoyed him but today there was no time to be upset.

He searched in the chest of drawers for the diary Grandma had sent him last Christmas. He found it beneath his swimming-costume. He pulled out the pencil from the slot on the spine and opened it at the month of July. The 22nd was his birthday. That was Saturday. Yesterday was the 23rd. Today was Monday, the 24th. That left forty-one days till the 2nd of September, the day when they returned to school. Five weeks and three days to save twenty-one pounds and eighty-five pence. If he couldn't do it by then, he might as well give up. A bike was no use in the dark winter evenings.

Brock wrote a large 1 against the 24th of July, and then numbered the days until he reached 41 at September the 2nd. Then he took his piggy-bank down from the window-ledge and emptied the money onto the bed. There were three one pound postal orders, a five-pound note, a ten pence piece and five pennies. That was right. Twenty-one pounds and eighty-five pence to save. Written on the blank page of the 22nd of July it appeared an awful lot of money. For a moment Brock's resolution wavered. But then he saw himself riding Whitman's bike and the gang asking for a ride. No, he wasn't giving in so easily.

He quickly pulled the blankets over the pillowcase. Dad made that rule last year. Brock had to see to his own bedroom in the holidays. Downstairs he found Mum reading the newspaper with a cup of tea in her hand.

'Hello, John,' she said. 'I didn't realize you were up.'

Brock brought a chair and sat down beside her. The house was quiet, as it always was on a Monday morning after Dad had gone to work. Having breakfast with Mum was one of the best things about the holidays.

'Mum,' Brock asked. 'Where are the newspaper shops in town?'

Mum poured them both a cup of tea and passed the sugar for Brock's cornflakes.

'Let me see now,' she answered. 'There's McIntyres in the Arcade. They deliver our papers. There's Malin's opposite the market, Bird's newsagency at the top of Tower Hill, and then there's that tobacconist next to Marks and Spencers, but I don't think they do very much business.'

She folded her newspaper inside out, lifted the cup to her mouth, and went on reading.

After several seconds she paused, and appeared to think.

'What did you want to know for?' she inquired.

'I've decided to save up and buy David Whitman's new racing-bike,' Brock explained excitedly. The words came out with a rush. He couldn't contain them. 'It's a secret though, so you mustn't tell Dad. Not yet at least. I'll have to sell my birthday bike. Nobody will buy it in its present condition, but if I paint the forks silver and the rest of the frame bright red it should be quite attractive. And I'll have to find myself a paper round.'

Brock's face was flushed as he finished.

Mum drank her cup of tea and placed it carefully on the saucer.

'You have had a lot of good ideas,' she replied with a smile. 'But if your birthday bicycle will be so nice when it's painted, why don't you keep it? Then there will be no necessity for you to save all that money. After all, you've only had your new bicycle for two days.'

Brock felt his heart sink as he listened to her words. His feelings must have been reflected in his face, because Mum hesitated before she continued speaking.

'And I don't suppose Dad would be very pleased for you to buy a bicycle from that boy, David Whitman,' she went on. 'If you really want to save thirty pounds wouldn't it be better to choose a new bicycle from one of those shops in town? It was only last week you told me that silver racing-bike was the one you really wanted.'

Brock might have guessed she would talk like this. She hadn't the faintest idea why his bike was like a tank, and it was no use trying to explain. She just didn't have the right sort of understanding. Yet he had to have her on his side. He couldn't make Dad change his mind, not on his own.

'I think you ought to ask Dad about the paper round,' Mum argued.

'But I've only forty-one days,' Brock told her frantically. 'I haven't a moment to lose.'

In the end she wouldn't say either yes or no, so Brock left in case she came to a decision and definitely said no.

'You be careful how you ride that bicycle through the traffic,' she called after him. 'And you ought to be thinking about your "Thank You" letters before very long.'

On the way to town Brock tried to think what he would say to the newsagents. He didn't find it easy, because he wasn't used to meeting strange people and asking them questions. He still hadn't made up his mind when he reached McIntyre's. He decided the best thing was to walk straight in. The right questions would come to him when he had to speak.

Brock was relieved to see there was only one man in the shop being served. A whole crowd and a long wait was what he had feared most. But then the unexpected happened. Instead of finishing with the other customer the shopkeeper spoke to Brock immediately.

'What do you want, sonny?' he asked sharply.

Brock lost his bearing. He began to speak but no words came into his mouth. His mind refused to function. Everything went blank.

'I – want – to buy – a bike,' Brock said.

'Well, you won't find one here,' the man told him. 'We sell newspapers and sweets.'

'I mean – I need a paper round – so as to save money – to buy a bike.' Brock managed to say the words, but it was not without a great deal of stuttering. 'You deliver our papers,' he said, hopefully.

'How old are you?' the shopkeeper demanded.

'Eleven,' Brock answered. 'It was my birthday last Saturday.'

'Then there's no job for you. You're too young – sorry.'

Brock turned and walked out of the shop. At the doorway he heard the shopkeeper say to the other man, 'Funny little lad.'

Brock nearly went straight home, but he had to pass Malin's so he thought there was nothing to lose. He leaned 'The Tank' against an advertisement sign. Before he went in he practised all the questions the other shopkeeper had asked him, and he whispered the answers to himself. This time he would be twelve years old.

He steeled himself for the ordeal and walked into the shop. There was nobody there but a woman behind the counter.

'I want to do a paper round,' Brock told her. 'Have you anything you can offer?'

'Where do you live?' the woman asked.

'3 Churchill Street,' Brock answered. He hadn't been expecting that question, but he'd managed all right.

'I've nothing at the present,' the woman said. 'But if you like to call back next month we might have something for you.'

Brock was back in the street before he realized she hadn't asked him his age.

And though he wasn't a paperboy he felt quite pleased with himself. He hadn't stuttered once. Nothing, nothing at all had gone wrong, except he still did not have a job. Brock hurried up Tower Hill. He didn't know exactly where Bird's Newsagency was, but there wasn't any trouble finding it. BIRD'S NEWSAGENCY was printed in big letters across the top of the shop.

Brock propped 'The Tank' against the pavement, drew a deep breath and pushed open the door. A bell jangled loudly above his head. There were footsteps to the rear. A curtain was pushed aside and a small bald-headed man with black horn-rimmed spectacles appeared in the opening. Brock liked him immediately, he liked his friendly smile, his large white teeth, and the top of his head, which shone as if it had been polished.

'And what can Mr Bird do for you, young fella?' he asked.

'I'm looking for a paper round,' Brock answered. The words came out fluently and naturally. It was partly because he had done it twice before, but it was also on account of Mr Bird's easy manner.

'Are you, indeed?' Mr Bird said, raising his eyebrows.

'Gladys,' he called. 'There's a young gentleman here to see us.'

The curtain parted a second time and a jolly-looking woman came towards Brock.

'Pleased to meet you, my young gentleman,' she said, holding her hand over the counter.

Brock shook hands with her. He felt quite bewildered. Everything was happening too quickly. But it was rather nice, not like the first shop.

'What's the young gentleman's name, Harold?' Mrs Bird asked.

'I forgot to inquire,' Mr Bird said.

'John,' said Brock. 'John Brockson.'

'He's after a paper round,' Mr Bird interrupted.

They both looked at each other and laughed.

'In that case he's come to the right place,' Mrs Bird said. 'Been wondering what we would do when Brian Anderson went on his holidays – this Friday it is.'

Brock felt his heart soaring. It almost fell when Mr Bird said he might be too young, but they agreed it would be all right, because Brock would only be with them for a few weeks.

'And what would a young gentleman like you be wanting a paper round for?' Mrs Bird asked.

'Well, it's like this,' Brock explained. 'I've just had a bike for my birthday – you can see it outside through the window. My Dad bought it – but it's not the one I wanted. It's an old Army bike – and all of my friends laugh at me, because it rattles and because I can't ride fast.' Brock paused and took a deep breath. He was being carried along by his own words.

'One of the gang – they're my friends – he has a white racing-bike and he says he'll sell it for thirty pounds.'

'And you want a paper round so you can buy this bike?' Mrs Bird asked.

'That's it,' Brock told her.

'Very good, too,' Mr Bird said. 'Can you start with the regular boy tonight?'

'Yes I can,' Brock burst in, before he had finished speaking.

'And there's mornings too,' Mr Bird went on. 'But they're six o'clock. A bit early for you I should think.'

'Don't worry,' Brock told him. 'I'll be there. You wait and see. I'll be there.' He turned at the doorway, waved to Mr and Mrs Bird, and then rushed out into the street.

Eight

It was market day and the town was beginning to be busy. Brock hummed to himself as he steered 'The Tank' between cars at the station traffic lights.

The tide is turning, Brock thought. From now on things will be all right for me. I have a feeling they will.

On the way out of town he bought two small tins of paint, one silver and one red. Together they cost one pound and twelve pence. Brock would have preferred not to spend any money, but if it really improved 'The Tank', then it would be worth it.

Before going home Brock called for Fagin. Fagin's seventeen-year-old stepbrother, Albert, opened the door. He said Fagin had just gone round to Brock's house. Fagin and Brock met each other at the bottom of Churchill Street.

'Guess what?' Brock called. 'I've been employed as a paperboy, starting tonight.'

Fagin was impressed. Brock had known he

would be. And he'd wanted to tell Fagin first, because Fagin was his best friend.

'Did you find out the wages?' Fagin asked.

'No,' Brock confessed. 'I forgot to do that.'

Fagin had finished his dinner, so he said he would come round to Brock's house and help with the painting.

Brock found a sheet of sandpaper on Dad's workbench. He tore it in two and together they sandpapered the old brown paint from 'The Tank'.

It took them almost an hour. When they had finished the concrete path was speckled with flecks of dry paint. They were rubbing the frame clean with a cloth when Mum knocked on the window. That meant dinner was ready. It was really annoying to break off when they were half way through the job. Still there was no use causing an argument. Delaying dinner was one thing which was certain to annoy Mum.

Brock glanced at his watch as he opened the kitchen door. It was twenty-five to two.

Mum put a plate of mince and potatoes in front of him. Brock ate as quickly as he could.

'John, will you sit up straight and eat your dinner properly,' Mum said severely.

Brock swallowed the food in his mouth, and then pulled his chair closer to the table.

'And just look at your hands. They're black,' Mum went on angrily.

'How many times do I have to tell you about washing before meals!'

Brock wiped his hands on his trousers.

'And that is not the way to do it,' she shouted.

After Brock came down from the bathroom Mum asked: 'You didn't by any chance find a paper round, did you?'

'Yes, I've got a job at Bird's Newsagency,' Brock told her, between mouthfuls. 'Starting tonight.'

'I wish you hadn't,' Mum said anxiously. 'I honestly don't know what Dad will say.'

'It'll be all right, Mum,' Brock told her. He didn't know whether it would be, but he hadn't time to worry about it now. In any case when Brock returned home from the shop, Mum would have told Dad all about it. Anyway, there wasn't a lot Dad could say. Brock only had fifty pence a week pocket money. Even Fagin was given more, and Clayton had a pound.

Brock pushed his plate away from him and stood up. He had reached the door when Mum called him back.

'I wonder if you'd mind washing the dishes?' she asked. Actually she was telling, not asking him.

'I'm terribly busy,' Brock told her.

'It'll only take you a minute,' Mum insisted.

'Why can't you do them?'

'I want to slip out to the shops.'

'I did them last week,' he argued.

'And I made the dinner last week.' She always gave that answer.

Brock knew he had to do them. It would be quicker than arguing any further. Noisily he carried the dishes over to the sink and washed them under the tap.

'And don't forget you have those "Thank you" letters to write sometime,' she reminded him, as he went out.

Brock slammed the door behind him.

He found Fagin cleaning the frame.

'I'll search for a brush,' Brock told him.

There was an old one in Dad's toolbox. Then he opened the tins of paint with the end of a chisel. They had just started when Whitman climbed over the fence.

'You'll only make it worse, painting a bike with a brush like that,' he sneered. 'You need a spray to do the job properly, and it takes an expert like me, who knows what he's doing.'

Fagin started the painting, while Brock screwed the bell onto the handlebars. 'The Tank' was looking better already.

Whitman was in a really horrible mood.

Brock said 'Thank you' for the bell, but Whitman wouldn't even smile, and of course he didn't help with the painting. He sat on the gate and lectured how he would have done it, while Fagin and Brock took it in turns with the brush. And the annoying thing was that Whitman was right. The brush had gone hard with tar which Dad had been using to mend the gutters. The red paint from the tin mixed with the tar and turned into a revolting, thick mud-coloured mixture. In places it stuck to the frame like treacle. Quite a lot of it dripped onto the concrete path. And then to finish everything Brock dropped red paint onto the forks, which Fagin had just painted silver.

Whitman climbed down from the gate. He took one last scornful stare at 'The Tank' and then walked off.

Brock could have sobbed. And everything had been going so well.

They cleaned up the mess as best as they could. Brock swilled the path with three buckets of water. The tar, the red and the silver paint all ran together. They used the old rags and the kitchen broom, but even when Brock half-closed his eyes the path was still the same muddy colour. Fortunately, Mum hadn't returned from her shopping, but when she did she was furious.

'Now this really is too bad, John,' she said, her voice quivering with emotion.

'Sorry,' Brock blurted out.

'It's no good being sorry afterwards,' she told him. 'You must think first in future.'

She made them start all over again with a pail of warm soapy water. She changed into old clothes and came out and helped them. Brock knew they were wasting their time. The paint was embedded in the concrete. Nothing would have removed it. After an hour's work it was hardly any different. Brock wished he could have asked Mum to leave it alone, but he sensed that the less he said the better. Mum was almost in tears. There was paint on Brock's trousers, the yard was a mess, and Mum's best broom was ruined. Brock really did feel sorry, but he knew it would be useless telling her so. Anyway he had troubles of his own. 'The Tank' was like one of those paintings they did at school. When Mum finally did let him go he was late for the paper round. And it was his first night. What would Mr and Mrs Bird think of him!

When he reached the newsagency, Brian Anderson was standing outside the shop with a bagful of newspapers over his arm. Brock held his chest and gasped for breath.

'You all right?' Brian asked him.

Brock closed his eyes and nodded his head.

'Here, take this then,' Brian told him, lowering the bag over Brock's shoulder.

Brock felt his knees begin to buckle beneath the weight. He held onto the wall and steadied himself.

'And you'll need this,' Brian said, handing him a card with the numbers and the names of the houses written on it.

There were only five streets but it seemed terribly confusing to Brock. It was all very well for Brian Anderson to say the numbers were written on the card. Brock couldn't understand which numbers belonged to which street. Brian had been doing the round for months. He knew it back to front. In any case he was fourteen years old. And he was so tall. He was taller than Whitman, almost as tall as Brock's Dad.

The thought of walking from house to house on his own frightened Brock. Some people came to their front doors. Brock wished he could say 'Good Evening' in that calm adult manner with which Brian Anderson spoke. Nothing seemed to be any effort to him.

Brian glanced at his watch as they returned to the shop. 'It took us nearly an hour tonight,' he said. 'Not bad considering you're a learner.'

Once Brian Anderson had gone Brock suddenly felt important. He was the only one of the gang who had a paper round. For once he'd done something before any of them. He'd completely forgotten about 'The Tank', the mess on the path, and Dad. As he walked home it all came back to him like an incredible unbelievable nightmare. He took his time, because if by chance there were visitors, Dad wouldn't be able to say anything while they were there. But there were no visitors and Dad was beside himself with rage. Brock had expected a row, but nothing to what took place.

'I've just about had enough of you,' Dad

shouted, as Brock walked through the door. 'I'd never have agreed to you having a bicycle if I'd have known there was to be this trouble.' He went on and on about the paint on the path, his best chisel and his only tar brush, which was now completely ruined.

And when Brock thought the row was over he started about the paper round.

'Do you realize it's against the law for a boy of your age to work?'

'No,' Brock mumbled, staring at the carpet.

'Well, you ought to then. And look at me – and take your hands out of your pockets when I'm talking to you. It will finish up with the police around here. And then what will you tell them?'

'I don't know,' Brock answered.

'Don't know! Don't know! In all my born days I've never met a child like you. You're getting too big for your boots. That's your trouble. If I'd taken a paper round without asking my father's permission I'd have been thrashed. Do you hear me! Thrashed!'

'A good job times have changed,' Brock told him. He didn't mean to say that. The words just came out on their own.

'What!' Dad shouted. 'What was that you said?' He blushed crimson. Even the bald top of his head went red.

At this point Mum intervened, and calmed him

down. She was a genius with Dad when he became upset. She made him sit down in his armchair, and read his newspaper. Then she led Brock into the kitchen, pulled a chair to the table and pushed him into it. Mollie scuttled from under the table. Mum placed a bowl of soup, a round of bread and an apple in front of him.

'Thank you,' Brock said. Mum stared at him with a mixture of anger and resigned exasperation.

'Just eat your tea,' she told him. 'Stay there, don't move, and don't say a word – not even to yourself. Do you understand?'

Brock raised his head, gave a quick nod, and then buttered his bread. He didn't look up again until Mum had returned to the dining-room.

'He'll finish up in serious difficulties if he continues in this manner,' Brock heard him say to Mum.

'He didn't mean to be disobedient,' Mum answered. 'He just didn't stop to think.'

'That's the whole trouble,' Dad told her.

'Yes, I know, but he is only eleven, Frank.'

'Only eleven, Mary. Age has nothing to do with it. That boy shows no consideration for other people.'

'You mustn't be too hard on him,' Mum said.

Dad started to answer her, but then he said no more.

Brock gulped down his soup and fled upstairs to

his bedroom. He went straight to the chest of drawers and took out his writing paper and envelopes. Standing at the window he wrote four 'Thank you' letters, one to Granny and Grandad in London, one to Grandma in Scotland, one to Auntie Margaret and Uncle Harold and one to Auntie Dot. He wrote the same for each letter, copying it out slowly and carefully in his very best handwriting, and when he had finished he tiptoed onto the landing and placed the envelopes on the carpet at the top of the stairs.

Then he undressed, switched off the light and climbed into bed. He waited for Mum to come to say good night. He waited and waited and after he had waited a very long time he knew that, for once, Mum wasn't coming to see him before he went to sleep.

Nine

For the second night running Brock slept badly. He could not get to sleep, no matter how hard he tried. He lay on his back, on his stomach, then on his side, but it made no difference. The bed became hotter and hotter, until it seemed like a raging inferno. Brock pushed the eiderdown to the floor with his feet.

He heard Mum making supper in the kitchen. Then there was talking. Brock guessed they were discussing him, but the conversation was too far away to hear.

Later Dad checked the doors to see if they were locked. Mum came ahead of him to bed. She hesitated at the top of the stairs. There was a rustle of paper. Brock knew she had picked up his 'Thank you' letters. After a long silence Mum took a long deep breath and sighed. Before she went into her own bedroom she put her head round Brock's door. Brock closed his eyes and pretended to be asleep. When he opened them she had gone away.

And then Brock started thinking about the difficulties of buying Whitman's bike. Once he'd begun he couldn't stop himself.

Life would be a great deal simpler if he made do with 'The Tank', he thought. The whole business was upsetting everybody. It was causing more trouble than it was worth. Halfway through the night he reached the decision not to buy Whitman's bike.

But then when morning approached, when the birds broke into song, when the darkness gave way to light, so Brock's conception of reality changed. It was always the same with Brock. He always finished up second best. Well, here was an opportunity for him to show the gang he was as good as any of them. And he could not allow that opportunity to slip through his fingers, whether Dad liked it or not.

When the clock in the hall struck five Brock went into the bathroom. It was going to be a beautiful day. Already the pearly white sky was changing to a pale blue. Brock ran cold water into the wash-basin. When it was full he ducked his head three times, but it didn't bring him to life. He still felt in a daze. And he had a horrible tight sensation in his stomach, as if a fist was gripping his insides. More than anything he wanted to sleep, but he didn't dare return to bed. If he dozed off he might not wake in time for the paper round.

He heard Dad turn over in bed and mumble

something to Mum. Brock dressed and escaped from the house before Dad came to see what he was doing. The paint on 'The Tank' was still sticky. Dust had settled all over it in the night, and dozens of tiny insects had been trapped by their wings and legs. When Brock took 'The Tank' out into the road it looked even worse than it had the previous afternoon. The red streak down the front fork had run into wavy lines with the silver paint. The result was an ugly patterned effect. Brock had hoped the streak might appear as though it was meant to be there, but it didn't. If he and Fagin had poured the paint straight from the tin it couldn't have been worse.

The newsagency wasn't open when Brock arrived at twenty past five. He stared into the silent interior at the light from the ice-cream box, which kept flickering on and off. It was nearly half an hour later when a van stopped, and the driver threw two bundles of newspapers into the shop doorway. Brock huddled on the step, and waited until Mr Bird opened the door at five to six.

'Good morning, young fella,' Mr Bird said. He seemed really pleased to see Brock so early.

When Brock admitted he hadn't had any breakfast, Mr Bird made a pot of tea for them both, and they sat on the high stools and sorted papers into different bags until the first men called on their way to work.

It was Brian Anderson who was late that morning. He was surprised to find Brock outside the shop with the board and bag ready. There weren't nearly so many papers as there had been the previous evening, and Brock managed a whole street on his own.

'You won't need the board by Friday,' Brian told him, when they returned to the shop.

'How's he coming along?' Mr Bird asked. He winked at Brock and squeezed his shoulder when Brian Anderson said he was making 'satisfactory progress'.

Scotty and Clayton were waiting for Brock when he reached home. They followed Brock into his yard and started making jokes about 'The Tank'.

'Where's this arrow lead to?' Clayton asked innocently, examining the streak down the front fork.

'Pointing to the centre of the earth,' Scotty added wisely. 'Attracted by gravity.'

In fact they were both jealous about Brock's paper round, because for once he'd thought of doing something before them. Clayton wanted to share the round but Brock refused.

'I'll have Fagin first if I need any help,' he told them.

Saying that annoyed them both. But they didn't call him 'Titch' that morning.

'How about a game of Monopoly?' Clayton suggested.

'Sorry,' Brock answered. 'I'm going to be much too busy today.'

'We'll take the set round to Raymond's house then,' Scotty said.

Brock thought for a moment.

'For five pence, you can,' he told them.

'You stingy little miser,' Clayton said incredulously – but he paid up nevertheless.

Brock didn't mind what they called him. It was another five pence to write in his diary. In any case, Clayton had plenty of money to buy a Monopoly set for himself. He went inside for the box and gave it to Clayton.

Mum told him not to rush off because breakfast was ready.

While he was eating his bacon sandwich Mum sat down beside him.

'I've something to tell you, John,' she began. 'And I'm afraid you're not going to like it.'

Brock didn't know what to expect.

'Dad has to attend a meeting in London,' she went on, speaking very quietly. 'A week next Friday, and he's arranged for us to accompany him. It's the only opportunity this year we'll have for a holiday.'

'How long for?' Brock asked.

'Three days. We'll be home on the Monday night.'

'I can't come,' Brock burst out.

'There's no use you talking like that, John.'

'I've my paper round to think of.'

'It's only three days. I'm sure they'd find someone else for a weekend.'

'I'm not coming I tell you,' Brock told her vehemently. 'I don't want to go to stupid old London.'

'Don't shout, John. Mrs Whitman will be able to hear every word you are saying.'

'I'm not coming,' Brock repeated. 'I'll stay here.'

'You can't do that.'

'Why not?' Brock demanded. 'Alan Scott did it last year.'

'Yes, I know dear,' Mum said softly. 'But Alan Scott did have Miss Stable to look after him.'

'Please, Mum, please,' Brock pleaded. 'Let me stay, please will you?' Mum turned away, rubbing the side of her cheek.

'I don't know, John,' she answered. 'I honestly don't know. I'll think about it. I'll have to work out how it might be arranged. Now you're not to set yourself any hopes. I truthfully can't imagine what Dad will say, not after the trouble we had last night.'

'Will you talk to him, Mum?'

'I'll talk to him,' Mum told him. 'I'll do my best, I promise I will.'

Brock was depressed all day. He couldn't remember feeling so depressed in his life before.

Every little thing he did was causing a disagreement. If they wanted to have a holiday in London, it was all right with him so long as they didn't expect him to go too. They were always saying they longed for a holiday by themselves. Well, here was their chance. He wasn't stopping them.

The gang played cricket that afternoon against Clayton's garage. Brock was out three times for a duck and he dropped the simplest of catches.

Mum wasn't in the house when he got home, so he didn't see her before his paper round.

'Is something the matter?' Mr Bird asked, when Brock walked into the shop.

Brock shook his head and picked up the bag.

'I just don't feel very well, that's all,' he told Mr Bird.

Brock dreaded going home, he dreaded walking through the door, most of all he dreaded another angry scene with Dad. Brock tried to prepare himself for the worst as he dragged himself up Churchill Street.

But then a miracle happened. That was the only possible way to describe it. In the first place Dad was not angry, which was the very last thing Brock expected.

'Sit down, John,' he said kindly. 'Eat your kipper before it goes cold.'

Brock obediently did as he was told. Mum poured out his tea.

'Your mother has been explaining to me about

the holidays,' Dad continued. He was speaking with slow deliberation, as if he was thinking of each word before he spoke it. Brock's heart seemed to miss a beat. 'I think it's a very good idea in the circumstances. I can see nothing whatsoever against it. We'll have to ask Mrs Whitman to keep an eye on you. Provided she says yes, I feel confident you're quite adult enough to take care of yourself for three days.'

Brock could hardly trust his ears. And as though that wasn't enough Dad said he would give Brock a pound to spend on whatever he wished, because he was staying at home and not coming with them.

'There, it's all settled then,' Mum said, smiling. 'Only haven't you anything to say?'

'Well – No – I mean – Yes – Thank you – Thank you very much indeed,' Brock answered in confusion. Brock looked into Mum's quiet smiling face and then he understood why Dad had suddenly changed. Mum must have talked to Dad, she must somehow have explained to him how much a racing-bike meant to Brock.

'Long as we're all happy,' Mum said with a laugh. 'I saw Miss Stable this afternoon and I took it into my head to ask her if she'd be willing for you to sleep at their house for the three nights while we're away. She said she'd be delighted and you were to go there for dinner and tea. So everything's taken care of.'

Brock would have preferred to have gone to

Fagin's, but what did it matter. Dad had let him do what he wanted – he'd allowed him to carry on with the paper round. And it was all because of Mum. It was Mum he had to thank.

That night Brock waited for her to come to his room, and when, at last, he heard her steps on the stairs, he prepared what he would say to her. But when she came through the door he could not find the words. She smiled gently, leaned over the bed and kissed him good night, and then she went from the room.

The days just slipped by. Mum made Brock have a 'lie down' after his morning round. Then it was dinner and hardly had he finished dinner when it was time to return to the shop. Mr Bird had put an advertisement in the window for the sale of 'The Tank', but so far there hadn't been any inquiries.

At the end of the first week, Mr Bird gave Brock three pounds, one pound fifty for the mornings and one pound fifty for the evenings. It was much more than Brock had expected to earn. When he wrote £3 in his diary on Saturday night, he had, deducting one pound and twelve pence for paint, ten pounds and fifty-eight pence. That was eight pounds and fifteen pence he had in the piggy-bank, five pence from Clayton, the three pounds wages and the fifty pence Dad always gave him on a Saturday morning. Brock had been afraid Dad might stop his pocket money because of the paper round – but he didn't. Dad said Brock had earned the money and he was entitled to it.

By the beginning of the second week Brock was used to delivering papers. The first ten minutes after leaving the shop was the only difficult time. The bag was so heavy with papers and magazines, it was like having a large stone tied round his neck. The red paint on 'The Tank' still wasn't hard, so Brock ran to the shop every day. He didn't want to take the risk of marking his clothes. Mum, Dad and himself were getting on so well together. He wanted to keep it that way. If things continued as they were, he might have Whitman's bike after all.

Ten

It was soon the following Friday. On the Thursday Mum cleaned the house from top to bottom. Brock couldn't understand her cleaning when she wasn't going to be there.

'It doesn't make any difference to me, Mum,' he told her, but she didn't take any notice. Then she began to worry about Mollie.

'You will look after her won't you, John?' she said.

'I'll see she's all right,' Brock promised.

'I'll ask Mrs Whitman to have her if you'd rather.'

'Don't bother,' Brock assured her.

'Long as you think you can remember her food.'

Brock had breakfast with them that Friday morning. He'd just returned from his paper round. They were both dressed in their best clothes, Mum in her purple dress, Dad in his navy blue suit.

'Now look after yourself, John,' Mum said. 'I shall be thinking of you. We'll be home about half past five on Monday and we'll see you then.'

Brock kissed her 'Good-bye'. She gave him a hug,

held him at arm's length and gazed into his eyes. And then the taxi arrived, which was a good job, because Brock knew Mum would have cried if it hadn't.

'Keep a look-out for Mollie,' she told him. 'I haven't seen her this morning. And I've ordered one bottle of milk a day so don't forget to drink it.'

'You'll be all right, son,' Dad said, running his hand through Brock's hair.

Brock watched the taxi disappear round the corner. Mum was waving to him from the rear window.

Brock went upstairs and brought his diary into the front room. This was the first occasion Brock had ever been left on his own. He could do exactly as he wanted, and nobody would be able to tell him otherwise.

Mum had left a pound note for Brock to buy anything he felt like, so there was no necessity for him to go hungry. And there was also the pound Dad had promised but Mum said she would keep it for him until they came back from London. Mum had written out Scotty's meal times on a postcard, and she'd stuck it to the mirror above the mantelpiece with a strip of Sellotape.

'Just in case you should forget,' she had told him. 'And remember not to be late.'

That first dinner at Scotty's, Brock felt shy and

embarrassed when he sat at the table. He wasn't used to eating at other people's houses, and he was frightened of Miss Stable because she was so stern and because she hardly ever smiled. Brock didn't know whether he should speak, but he was too nervous, so he just sat and said nothing.

Fortunately, Clayton called for them and Miss Stable said they could go out and play. Clayton was really nasty to Brock. He pushed Brock into Scotty's greenhouse and locked him inside. He'd have left him there if Brock hadn't shouted – 'Help' – as loud as he could.

After they let him out Brock ran home without speaking to them. Mrs Whitman called to him from the upstairs window.

'Is there anything you need, John?'

'No, thank you,' Brock told her.

'If there's anything whatsoever just let me know.'

'Yes, I will,' Brock said. 'I'm all right, thank you.'

Mrs Whitman smiled and closed the window.

Brock picked up the bottle of milk from the front doorstep, and as he did so Mollie came running from under the hedge. She miaowed appealingly to be let in. Brock opened a tin of cat food and scraped it out onto her dish. She rubbed her head against his legs and purred all the time. Then she ate it, while Brock stood and watched her.

There wasn't a mark on her dish when she had finished.

Brock went into the living-room and picked up his diary. Before he could open it, Mollie had jumped onto his knee. She pushed her paws up and down on his chest, and at the same time she rubbed her head against Brock's face. He had never heard her purr so loudly.

Brock had been up since six o'clock. What with the excitement of Mum and Dad going, he felt tired, so he decided to lie down before his evening round. He pushed off his shoes and snuggled into the settee cushions. Mollie lay beside him and fell asleep almost immediately. But Brock didn't find it easy to relax with the house being so quiet.

Once he drifted into a half-sleep, but the wind woke him again. Suddenly, he was wide awake, his heart beating like a sledge-hammer. There was a noise from the kitchen. Brock was certain there was somebody outside the door with his ear to the keyhole. He imagined it was a man with a black patch over his eye and a dagger in his hand. Brock desperately wanted to scream or call for help, but he didn't dare move. He lay as still as a mouse and held his breath.

Suddenly a loud knocking came at the kitchen door. Mollie tugged her claws loose of Brock's jumper and shot under the table. Brock struggled to his feet and went to see who it was. He needn't have worried, because it was only the breadman. After that Brock opened the bottle of milk. He drank it in one go straight from the bottle. Then he went round to Fagin's and they played French cricket until it was time for Brock to leave for his paper round.

Brock came to know Mr and Mrs Bird even better while Mum and Dad were away. After finishing his round Brock stayed talking at the shop.

'It's most considerate you giving up your holidays just for us,' Mr Bird told him. Mrs Bird made Brock a hot drink before he went to Scotty's, and once they gave him a large packet of licorice allsorts.

Brock explained to Mr and Mrs Bird about his savings and the diary. They were really interested in anything he had to tell them.

Afterwards Brock went back to Scotty's, but he never hurried, because Clayton was always there. Clayton would wait in the garage till they had eaten their tea. When they came out an argument would have started if Brock had stayed with them. Instead Brock went to the room Miss Stable had arranged for him. It was next to Scotty's bedroom, but if Scotty wasn't playing with Clayton, then he was reading his books, so Brock hardly saw anything of him. Brock didn't mind, because by evening he was so worn out, that he was glad to be able to go straight to bed. Anyway he had to get up each morning at a quarter to six. Dad had lent him his alarm-clock so he wouldn't oversleep.

On the Monday a postcard came from London. Mum said they were having a nice time, and she hoped he was getting on all right. On the other side of the card was a coloured photograph of a racing bike, but it wasn't as good, not nearly as good as Whitman's bike.

All that day Brock was excited, because Mum and Dad were due back at half past five. After dinner Brock thanked Miss Stable for having him. Then he went home and tidied his bedroom. After that he arranged all the newspapers and letters in a pile at the bottom of the stairs and then he pushed the pound note through the slot in his piggy-bank, and he wrote on a piece of paper,

3 bars of chocolate
2 pockets of potatoe crisps
bag of sweets [licorice allsorts
2 bottles of lemonade
4 icecream
~~apples~~

Syned
John

That ought to be about right to have spent it all. He thought he had remembered everything. Looking at himself in the mirror, he decided to wash his face and comb his hair. It was one thing Mum never missed. It was still only half past three, so he went to Fagin's on 'The Tank'. They had races round the block until Brock had to leave for his paper round.

Eleven

It was raining when Brock finished the evening round, but he didn't shelter in the shop. He handed the bag to Mr Bird and said,

'My mum and dad are coming home at half past five.' He stopped at the door to let a customer pass him. Then he jumped on 'The Tank' and rode home as fast as he could.

There was no sign of them coming up Churchill Street, but when Brock passed the front window he saw they had arrived before him. He dropped 'The Tank' on the curb and ran in through the kitchen door.

'Hello,' they both said together.

'Hello,' Brock answered smiling.

Not until that moment did he realize how he had missed them. They were dressed in the same clothes they had left in. And the suitcases were placed by the side of the fireplace. Mum had Mollie in her arms, but when Brock came into the room she put the cat down and gave him a kiss. And when she kissed him Brock kissed her back. Normally he didn't like kissing, but today was different, because there was nobody else in the room, and because Mum had been away for three days. He was really glad to see them. He liked just being in their presence. He couldn't remember feeling like that before.

'What awful weather it's been,' Mum said. 'Though the hotel made up for it. The meals were absolutely delicious. You could have had fish and chips and ice-cream every meal if you'd been with us.'

'How's your paper round been?' Dad asked.

'All right, thank you,' Brock answered.

'Oh, we missed you, John,' Mum said. 'Everywhere we went I kept on looking for you. I just couldn't get used to you not being with us. That's true isn't it, Frank?'

'It is, Mary,' Dad agreed.

'And we went to so many different places,' Mum explained excitedly. 'Buckingham Palace, Westminster Abbey, the Houses of Parliament. You would have enjoyed it, you really would. We were ever so sorry you couldn't come.' For one single moment Brock wished he had gone, but it was only a moment, for then he thought of the money and Whitman's bike.

'We bought this for you,' Mum said, opening one of the suitcases. She took out a red jumper with a picture of a racing-bike across the front of it. Brock couldn't have chosen a better present himself. It was just as good as Whitman's white track-suit, better in fact.

'It's exactly what I wanted,' Brock told them.

'We thought you would appreciate it,' Mum said. 'And were your meals all right?'

'Yes, thank you,' Brock told her, pulling the jumper over his head.

'Long as you had enough to eat. And what time you went to bed – I'd better not ask.'

'Half past seven,' Brock informed her, rolling down the collar.

'Did you indeed! I must ask Miss Stable the secret.' Mum adjusted the bottom of the jumper, and picked off some fluff with the ends of her fingers. Then she straightened his hair with the palm of her hand.

'Oh, doesn't he look handsome, Frank?'

'Yes, most attractive,' Dad answered, though in fact he wasn't paying attention.

They were nicer to him the week after they returned from the holidays, than they had ever been before. On the Tuesday night Dad came into Brock's bedroom, which was a thing he normally never did. Brock had cleaned his teeth, and he was reading a comic before turning off the light. He heard Dad's footsteps on the stairs, but he was so engrossed in the comic, that he didn't take any

notice. He got a shock when there was a knock at the door, and then Dad came in. Dad smiled at Brock and sat on the bed beside him.

'Mum and I have been discussing your bike,' Dad said suddenly. 'I mean the bike I bought for your birthday.'

'Yes,' Brock answered timidly.

'I understand it's not the bike you want,' Dad said.

'No,' Brock told him.

'Well, if Whitman's bike is what you're after, then it's not for me to stand in your way. But I wish to say one thing, and that is if you are to have a racing-bike, then you will have to promise to be very careful.'

'I promise,' Brock said hurriedly.

'That's a good boy. And there's one other thing before I forget. I'd rather you didn't sell the bike we gave you for your birthday. I'll give you the twelve pounds I paid for it, and then if my own breaks down I can use it to get to work. How does that arrangement suit you?'

'All right, thank you,' Brock said.

'Good, I hoped it might.'

Brock dropped the comic onto the carpet and snuggled down into the bedclothes. Dad turned off the light at the door and went out.

'Good night,' Dad called from the landing.

'Good night,' Brock answered.

*

The dream of Whitman's bike had suddenly become a reality, and it was Dad who had made it possible. Without Dad's twelve pounds he might never have had enough money. Now it was all going to work out as he had planned. Brian Anderson would return to his paper round the following Saturday. By then Brock would have the thirty pounds he needed to buy Whitman's bike.

On the Thursday of that week Fagin told Scotty and Clayton about Brock's plan. By the evening Whitman knew as well. Brock was annoyed with Fagin because he had broken the secret. Clayton said Brock ought to be grateful to Fagin, because otherwise Whitman might have sold the bike to someone else.

'I don't believe he's got the money,' Whitman said.

'You wait until Saturday,' Brock told him. 'You wait and you'll see.'

Finally it was Saturday night. Brock completed the paper round for the last time. Mr Bird gave Brock his wages, and an extra thirty pence to go with it.

'That's our contribution towards your new bike,' Mr Bird explained. 'One penny for every pound your new bike will cost.'

'We shall miss him won't we, Harold?' Mrs Bird said. Mr Bird agreed that they would.

'You bring your new bike to show us,' Mr Bird told him.

'I will,' Brock said. 'As soon as I've got it.'

Brock rode home on 'The Tank'. This was to be the last time he would ride it. He had hated 'The Tank' deeply, and it had caused him so much unhappiness, but now it was to be Dad's, Brock suddenly felt an affection for its massive cumbersome form.

As soon as he got in the house, he went to his bedroom, and added up his money. It was all written down in the diary. Altogether it came to thirty-one pounds and eighty-eight pence. He didn't actually have the money. Mum was keeping it safe for him in her old biscuit tin, just in case a burglar broke into the house. It was only asking for trouble leaving that much money lying about.

Brock went downstairs and gave Mum the wages. She took out the old biscuit tin and emptied Brock's savings onto the table. When he counted it there was fifty pence short.

'Where is it?' Brock demanded.

'Now, I remember,' Mum said. 'Dad borrowed it last week when he was in a hurry. He must have forgotten to put it back.'

'Well, I must have it by the morning, because I'm buying David Whitman's bike,' Brock told her.

Mum was silent for several seconds. Then she said, 'Are you quite sure it is what you want?'

'We've been through all this before, Mum,' Brock explained impatiently. 'The frame is extra light, and it's been built by hand, not on an assembly line, like these bikes in the shops. I've ridden it myself and I know – it's perfect in every way.'

'I see,' Mum answered with a resigned sigh. She turned back to the stove. 'Be sure that boy doesn't come round to our house early tomorrow morning,' were her last words.

Brock walked into the dining-room without answering.

It was still early, but Brock didn't feel like playing with the gang. He didn't want to see any of them until he had Whitman's bike. Instead he went to his room and took the diary from under his pillow. The cover was creased, and the pages were wrinkled and dirty from being handled so much. Brock remembered the morning when he'd first opened the diary. It seemed far away, seemed to belong to another period in time.

Brock put a large star against Sunday, August the 13th. That was tomorrow. By tomorrow he would have achieved the impossible – he would have realized his dream. By tomorrow he would have Whitman's bike. The thirteenth was his lucky day – it would be Brock's day.

He lay on the bed, and closed his eyes. He thought of all the things he would do with Whitman's bike. How happy he would be when the bike belonged to him. Nobody would be able to take it from him. Tomorrow he'd be as good as Scotty and Clayton – and Whitman too. How happy it would make him. Judith might decide to come out with him now he was to have a good bike. And he would probably enter for races. If he won he would be asked to travel all over the world. Who could say what the future held for him! He imagined himself with a garland of flowers round his neck, walking down the steps from a jet airliner, answering questions into a barrage of microphones, and being kissed by Judith at the same time. And there were several television cameras and crowds of people trying in vain to catch a glimpse of him.

He must have fallen asleep, because the next thing Brock knew Mum was leaning over him in the dark chill air.

'You'll have to change into your pyjamas,' she was telling him.

Brock could hear the television downstairs. In a daze he fumbled with his buttons and then tumbled into bed. He fell asleep almost immediately, and dreamt of riding to the Tilburn Hills on Whitman's bike. He was wearing a white track-suit over his new jumper and blue jeans. A long peaked cap was pulled down low over his eyes.

Twelve

It was a perfect summer's day. At eight o'clock in the morning the air was fresh and cool. The bright sun had almost dried the patterns of moisture from Brock's bedroom window.

Whitman woke him by climbing the drainpipe and banging on the windowpane. Brock had his back to the window. Two or three times he heard knockings in his dream, but it wasn't until Whitman had nearly cracked the glass with his fist that Brock turned over and saw Whitman hanging onto the drainpipe. His nose was pressed flat against the pane.

It was all Brock could do to keep him quiet. He knew the instant he opened the window Whitman would be in his room.

'Have you got the money?' Whitman demanded. His voice echoed down the empty street.

Brock made signs with his hands for him to go away, but Whitman wouldn't take any notice.

'I'll see you in half an hour,' Brock whispered.

'What!' Whitman shouted.

'I'll see you in half an hour,' Brock repeated in a voice as loud as he dared.

Whitman still didn't hear.

Luckily Mrs Fox in the house opposite came out for her milk. She looked up and called: 'What are you doing up there, young man?'

Whitman slid down the drainpipe onto the porch, and jumped to the ground. Brock saw him disappear round the side of the house.

Fortunately the noise hadn't woken Dad. At any rate Mum didn't complain when she got up to make Dad's breakfast at a quarter to nine.

When Brock asked for his thirty pounds Mum said the bike would have to be brought to the kitchen door first. Brock found Whitman climbing up and down the lamp-post on the green. He went wild when Brock gave him Mum's instructions.

'I've a good mind not to sell you the bike,' he said, angrily. But after a lot of shouting about what queer people Brock had for parents, he brought the bike into Brock's back yard.

Brock went into the kitchen and told Mum they were ready.

Immediately Whitman's attitude completely changed.

'It's a very good bike,' he told Mum. 'The frame is made from special light alloy, and there's a speedometer, which tells how fast you are travelling. I fitted that only last week. And I've lowered the seat so it will be just right for John.'

Mum didn't say anything. She looked at Brock, started to speak, and then shrugged her shoulders instead. She opened the cabinet above the sink and took down the old biscuit tin. Her lips were pressed tightly together as she counted out the money. She replaced the postal orders with pound notes from her own purse.

'And you will need to be careful with the brakes,' Whitman warned. 'They're very finely adjusted.' He took the money from Mum's hand and then he was gone.

Brock followed him into the yard. The bike was leaning against the wall. Brock could hardly believe it. For three weeks he'd dreamed and planned this moment. Now it was happening. It was like a fairy-tale come true. Now the bike was his. It belonged to him. It was like no other bike in the world. Hadn't Whitman said so? Brock sucked his lower lip, as he felt a surge of feeling, like an electric current, pass through his body.

This is the turning point in my life, Brock thought. I know it is. From today things *will* be different for me.

The sun glinted on the white frame and the silver wheel rims, throwing dazzling star shapes into Brock's face. He ran his fingers along the handlebars down to where the ends were bound in white towelling. The saddle was so slim – and the treads on the tyres were thick and prominent – and the white translucent mudguards – and the alloy gear-lever screwed to the angled part of the frame, which changed the five gears on the back wheel. And – and – and just everything about the bike. Brock couldn't bear to take his eyes from it. He went to the fence close to Mr Whitman's garden, he climbed on the gate, and then he went into the road. From every position the bike was perfect, so perfect he was almost afraid to ride it. He turned the bike upside down and wiped several specks of dust from the underside of the saddlebag. Even upside down it was the perfection of creation.

Turning it right way up he wiped the saddle and handlebars, where they had touched the ground, though Brock had been so careful that there wasn't even the trace of a mark or a scratch. He went into the kitchen and found Mum washing the breakfast dishes.

'Do you need anything in town?' he asked her.

Mum paused.

'I don't think there is, John,' she told him. 'I did all my shopping on Friday.'

'What about matches?' Mum nearly always forgot to buy matches.

'Yes, you could fetch two boxes,' Mum said smiling. 'Although I'm afraid there isn't anything else I need.'

Brock was glad there was something, for he

wanted to show her how pleased he was, that it was Whitman's bike and no other. He took the ten pence piece from her and started for the door.

'What about your breakfast?' Mum said.

'I had some bread and butter and a glass of milk before you got up,' Brock lied. He couldn't bear the thought of being delayed from his first ride.

The sun was warm and the street was bathed in a strong clear light. There were insects in the air and a bee buzzed around the roses on the front porch. Brock felt peaceful and in complete control of himself as he wheeled the bike onto the road. Mrs Fox was watching him from her window. Brock would not have been surprised if the whole street had come out to see him off. He propped the bike against the curb and climbed on. Then he was off. The slightest of breezes pressed against his face. It was deliciously pleasant.

The bike was completely silent except for the ticking of the rear cogs. It was how he remembered it the day they had been to the Tilburn Hills. A sense of freedom returned to him as he sped forward without any effort. Yet it was different today, for now the bike was his. He could sit on the saddle, now that it had been lowered. Now the whole world stretched in front of him.

Over the level-crossing he saw one of the boys from his class. The boy turned and stared as Brock flashed past him. Brock waved a hand to him as he overtook a bus, which slowed down for two children waiting at the next stop.

I won't be travelling on any buses, Brock thought. Not ever again. He arrived at Bird's newsagency in less than seven minutes. With 'The Tank' it had taken at least a quarter of an hour.

'So this is the bike,' Mr Bird said, as Brock led him out of the shop door. 'It's a beauty and there's no mistake.' Mrs Bird came out too. She admired it, not as much as Mr Bird had, but Brock decided that was on account of her being a woman. But they both understood what the bike meant to him.

'We're proud of you, the same as if you were our own son,' Mr Bird told Brock. Then a customer arrived, so they couldn't stay talking any longer. Just in time Brock remembered the boxes of matches. They all had a laugh, that Brock had come into town, and he'd almost forgotten the matches.

It was the best bike in the world, Brock thought as he rode home. The best bike in England, Scotland, Ireland, Wales, in Europe, Africa, Asia, Australia and the whole of America too. Yes, sir, the best bike in the whole world. There isn't another one like it.

'How much would you sell it for?' a man was asking him.

'It's not for sale,' Brock told him.

'Forty pounds,' the man said.

'Sorry,' Brock answered. 'It's not for sale.'

'Four hundred pounds?'

'Not four hundred, four thousand, four million, four billion, four trillion, four trillion million million million,' Brock sang at the top of his voice. Two old ladies stared in amazement as Brock sped past them. He raised both hands in the air, turned in his seat, and winked at them. Then he pedalled even faster, continued singing, then he changed the singing to yodelling. He was so happy, he didn't care who saw him, didn't care what anybody thought.

He took a detour home, but he still arrived in Churchill Street too soon.

'Stand aside, here comes Brockson,' Brock shouted. He applied the brakes, jumped off and carried the bike into the back yard. He spent the rest of the morning polishing the spokes and wheel rims. It was no effort, and when he was finished, the bike glistened and sparkled even brighter than before.

When Mum called him he asked her if he could have his dinner on the kitchen table.

'If you really want to,' she answered.'But whatever for?'

'Because I want my bike near me,' Brock told her. 'Beside my chair.'

'I'm afraid you can't do that,' she said.

'Well, can I leave the door open?'

'No, you cannot,' Mum replied. 'I don't want the whole street staring into my kitchen.'

Brock knew there was no use saying any more, not in any argument with Mum when it was about her kitchen. He ate his dinner quickly and it was a good job he did, because he had hardly finished when there was a sound of voices from the back yard. Somebody was touching his bike. Brock leapt to his feet and rushed outside. It was Scotty and Clayton. They both had their hands on his bike.

'Get off it,' Brock told them roughly.

'All right, Titch, all right,' Scotty said, standing back.

'Give us a ride,' Clayton said in a pleading voice.

'Sorry,' Brock told them. 'I've decided not to allow anybody.'

'You tight-fisted little toad,' Clayton retorted indignantly. Brock was unmoved.

'I'll give you a race instead,' he suggested. Neither of them answered.

'Ten times round the block and you both have half a block start.'

'Listen to the champion,' Clayton sneered.

'You're only jealous,' Brock said.

Clayton and Brock stared at each other belligerently.

'Thirty pounds is what you paid,' Scotty observed.

'What if it was?' Brock asked. He was becoming tired of them both. They were spoiling his day.

'He offered it to me for twenty,' Scotty said.

'Did the same with me,' Clayton added.

'You're lying,' Brock replied.

'Suit yourself,' Scotty said calmly. 'Only I wouldn't buy it because the forks are out of line.'

'You're jealous,' Brock shouted. They were upsetting him now.

'I noticed that as well,' Clayton said. 'Could be dangerous, Alan, I suppose?'

'Absolutely,' Scotty agreed.

He didn't believe them, but after they had gone, he peered down the line of the frame with one eye closed, and it did seem to Brock the forks were ever so slightly twisted. Or was it his imagination? He could not be certain. What if they were right? If there was an imperfection, it might cause him to crash. Brock had a horrific vision of his bike being squashed by a steam-roller, of it being pressed flat. The wheels and the frame would be distorted and twisted. Brock shuddered. He could not bear to think of the possibility.

But he soon forgot these thoughts when he took his bike out into the street again. He rode round and round the block, one hundred and thirty-seven times. On the one hundred and thirty-eighth lap

Fagin came to call for him so he had to stop. Fagin thought the bike was as marvellous as Brock did, and he wasn't jealous like Scotty and Clayton had been.

'I'm sorry I can't give you a ride,' Brock explained. 'But I've refused the other two and it's only right to make the same rule for everybody.'

Fagin looked so disappointed, Brock thought he was going to cry.

'I'll think again, next week,' Brock promised. 'And you'll be first, I promise. You're my best friend.'

'I understand,' Fagin said, though it was obvious he didn't, because afterwards he went straight home, and he didn't say good-bye, which was unusual for Fagin. Brock wondered for a moment if he'd been mean, but it was only for a moment. The next instant he was racing round the block, trying to beat a two hundred lap record.

After tea Brock wheeled his bike onto the green, and leaned it against the lamp-post in the quietness of Sunday evening. He lounged in the long grass, hidden from view, and watched people going by in their best clothes. One couple walked right across the green, and the man stared at Brock's bike as he went past. Brock smiled to himself, chewed a strand of grass, and then began making a daisy chain. He waited for somebody else to admire his bike and when nobody came, he finished the daisy chain, draped it over the handlebars; and then he went home for a bath.

He lay for ages in the warm water and planned all the different places he would visit. London was a hundred and eighty miles away. He'd probably go there next year or the year after. The rest of the gang could come as well if they wanted. He might even lend Whitman 'The Tank'. From now on it wouldn't be Brock who'd be left behind in the mist.

That night Brock stayed in his room. He took out his paints and made a picture of Whitman's bike. No – not Whitman's bike. It was – Brock's bike now. It took him two hours and it was the best painting he had ever done. The bike filled the whole paper, and standing to one side was a tall figure dressed in a track suit with BROCKSON printed on his back. When the painting was finished and dry, Brock attached it to the wall with four pins. Straightaway he took it down again, because it was crooked and because he wanted it next to the bike posters. The second time he did it perfectly. Then he lay on his bed with his hands behind his head and admired it until Mum came upstairs to say good night.

'It's my masterpiece,' Brock told her.

'I'm not so sure about your masterpiece,' Mum replied doubtfully. 'But I agree it's one of the best paintings you've ever done.'

'Mum,' Brock called, as she closed his bedroom door behind her. Her footsteps faltered.

'What is it now, John?' she demanded wearily. Her voice was flat and emotionless.

'Is the wash-house locked?' Brock asked.

'I expect so,' she answered. 'Dad always sees to it last thing before he goes to bed.'

'Will you check it now?' Brock pleaded.

Mum took a long breath.

'Oh, all right, John, only it's time you were asleep.'

Brock listened as her feet padded on the stairs, then there was the jangling of the loose kitchen door handle. Several seconds later, the wash-house door banged and there was a grating sound as the key was turned in the lock.

'What are you doing?' Brock heard Dad say.

Mum's reply was muffled and inaudible. Then she was speaking again. They must have moved nearer because Brock could hear clearly.

'He's so happy with his new bike, Frank,' Mum said.

'I am pleased,' Dad replied.

'I think it's done him the world of good,' Mum went on. 'He's painted this picture of a bike and he told me it was his masterpiece.'

Dad laughed at this and Mum laughed with him.

Brock heard footsteps. Their voices faded away.

Brock moulded the bedclothes around his body, made himself comfortable and then closed his eyes. His sleep was sound and peaceful that night.

Thirteen

The next day was Monday. It was one of those blustery days in mid-August when suddenly the first signs of autumn are present. It was much colder than it had been for several weeks, and the rain, which fell intermittently all day, was cheerless and cold.

Mum made Brock put on an extra sweater, but he still kept his bike jumper on top. The jeans and the jumper were what he would always wear for his bike.

That afternoon, in between showers, the gang played cricket in Clayton's driveway. It was one of the best games of the whole summer. Brock scored a faultless half-century. He declared when he was fifty-three, and straight afterwards he clean-bowled Scotty and Clayton with consecutive balls. Then, in the next over, he had Whitman caught at silly mid-on. Brock had never played like this in his life before. He couldn't do anything wrong.

'Take it easy,' Fagin told him, as he took up the bat.

Brock cart-wheeled back to his run, raced to the wicket, and flung down the ball.

Fagin lunged forward. The ball struck the shoulder of the bat, and rebounded.

Brock dived low across the lawn and took the catch close to the ground.

Fagin threw down the bat and walked to his fielding position. For the rest of the afternoon he didn't speak another word to any of them.

It was Brock's innings again and he hit five fours and a six, before rain stopped play.

'I'll take you all on tomorrow – by myself,' Brock told them, as he did a hand-stand against the garage door.

'You needn't think you're that big,' Clayton shouted.

'Try not to be jealous,' Brock answered.

He left them all sheltering from the rain in Clayton's garage. Fagin stayed with them, which was most unlike Fagin. Normally he wouldn't do anything without Brock.

It was after five when Brock opened the kitchen door. Mum hadn't even laid out the cups and saucers for tea. She was sitting at the table wrapping up a parcel. She said it was Grandad's birthday the day after tomorrow, and if the parcel wasn't posted right away, Grandad might not have it for Wednesday.

'Be a good boy and post it for me,' Mum asked.

Brock was aching all over from the game of cricket, but he couldn't let her down after all she'd done for him, even though it would mean riding the mile and a half to town. Still it wouldn't take long on his new bike.

'Hadn't you better take a coat?' Mum called. 'It was raining only a few minutes ago.'

'I'll be all right,' Brock replied indifferently.

The parcel was too large for the saddle-bag so he had to carry it with one hand. He timed himself by his wrist-watch and reached the post office in six minutes and forty-five seconds. His fastest speed on the speedometer was 19 mph. While waiting to be served he decided to try and beat this time on the return journey. It ought to be easy because he wouldn't have the parcel to carry and going back the wind would be in his favour.

He stood astride the bike by the side of the road. He waited till the second hand was approaching the twelve. Then he counted five, four, three, two, one – zero. He was off. On the hill out of town he caught up with a bus and stayed close behind it to the next stop. As he came over the hill he was doing 15 mph. His time was one minute and twenty-four seconds. He was out of town and into the countryside now. There would no longer be any need to slow down for traffic. He changed into second gear. A hundred yards further on he was in top. He was travelling at 21 mph. His time was two minutes and twenty seconds. His feet moved powerfully round and round. The wind behind helped him on. There was only him, the wind, the bike and the road. Everything else had ceased to exist.

Then he was in a race, and there were crowds of people standing in the fields, peering over the hedgerows. There were cars with loudspeakers, cars with cameras, and one car with a commentator.

'And what a great race it's been for this brilliant young lad, John Brockson,' the man was shouting excitedly. 'His first trial on this remarkable white racing-bike built by that famous mechanic, David Whitman. Nobody would have given this boy a chance and yet here he is in fifth place with one mile still to go. And at this very moment an amazing thing is happening. Brockson is coming up on the outside – he's passed Dolci, the Italian champion. Now he's gaining on the American No 1, Mechelson – and he's overtaken Mechelson. Brockson is in third place with three quarters of a mile to go. Can he do it? We're in the final straight and it's downhill all the way. He's coming up behind the Swede, Lindgren. Lindgren is doing everything he can – but Brockson is level with him – and Brockson is in front. Brockson has overtaken Lindgren. There's only Whitman the English wizard mechanic between Brockson and victory.

Brockson is closing in fast. Whitman is looking behind him. He's seen Brockson. Whitman is making a tremendous spurt – he's making a desperate effort to stay in front – but Brockson is travelling faster. It looks as if Brockson will be too good for him. Brockson must be travelling at more than 25 mph at this very moment. The crowd are going wild. They're shouting, "Brockson – Brockson – Brockson". What a race it's been for this boy. But can he do it? Can Whitman hold onto his slender lead? There's less than a quarter of a mile to the finishing post. And Brockson has passed him on the inside. Brockson has passed him. Whitman is appealing for an infringement, but it won't make any difference, Brockson is streaking ahead. He's left Whitman standing. One more corner and the championship will be his. The sweat is literally pouring down Brockson's face. He must be very tired. But he's smiling and he's lifting his hand to the crowd, acknowledging the support they have given him. What a fantastic race this has been, Ladies and Gentlemen. Who could have predicted that we would have a new world champion – John Brockson from England.'

The road bends sharply as it enters the village. Brock was doing 28 mph as he came round the corner. It was the fastest speed he had ever done. The road and the hedgerows streaked towards him in a frightening manner. The Queen was presenting

Brock with a silver plate, which caught dazzling reflections from the sun, and at the same time Judith was kissing him on the cheek. Whitman was standing in the background, a defeated expression on his face. His trainer, Brian Anderson, was doing his best to console him.

Brock didn't see the parked van until the very last moment. He swerved into the middle of the road. It was the only way to avoid crashing into the van. Unfortunately for him a car was coming round the corner in the opposite direction. Brock experienced terror as, suddenly, he was brought back to reality. He jammed on the brakes with all the strength he possessed. The bike wobbled and then reacted violently. It skidded on a wet patch of road where the rain had not dried. Everything went out of control. Almost on top of him, there was a terrible screeching of car brakes. It seemed as close as when somebody shouts in one's ear. The bike slowed down but then it stopped dead. Brock was catapulted into the air. He was being thrown upwards. He grasped with his hands, but there was nothing to hold. In that brief fraction of a second he remembered Whitman's warning.

'You will need to be careful with the brakes. They're very finely adjusted.'

Then his body was jarred with a heavy fall. For an instant he felt sick, but the next moment the nausea had passed. He was lying on soft wet grass.

The wetness was against his face, and there was a jabbing pain in one leg. For several seconds he lay in a daze. A door slammed somewhere quite near by. A man came running towards him.

'Are you all right?' the man was saying. 'Speak to me if you can.' He sounded very nervous. He was holding Brock with his hands, feeling him all over.

Brock grasped the man's jacket and struggled to his feet.

'My bike,' Brock gasped frantically. 'Where's my bike?' It was all he could think of.

'It's over here, laddie. Not much harm done by the look of things.'

The man took Brock by the arm and led him to the other side of the road. Brock could not understand how he'd been on one side of the road and the bike was now on the other. It had been thrown into the hedge and was lying upside down among a tangle of brambles, old newspapers and tin cans. The front wheel revolved in mid-air, carried on by its own momentum. The saddle-bag must have been torn loose in the crash for it lay on its own in the grass.

The man freed the bike from the hedge and set it upright. The saddle was facing back to front, the handlebars were twisted upside down. They looked grotesque in that position. One of the pedals was deformed and clotted with mud, but

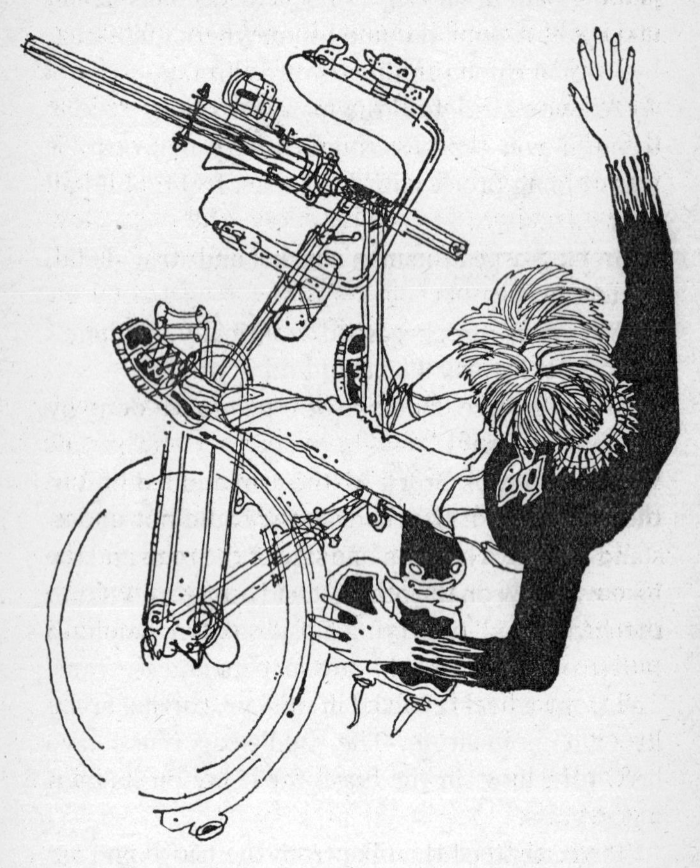

worst of all, down one side of the frame, the white paint was scraped off. It was as if somebody had taken a knife and drawn it along the metal tubing.

Brock stood motionless, unable to comprehend what he saw before his eyes. It seemed incredible that this was the same bike, his bike, for now it was no longer perfect. Only a minute before it had been a balance of beautiful curves and lines. Now it was nothing more than a collection of metal, rubber and leather. He continued to stand by his bike, oblivious of his surroundings, unaware of what was happening.

Brock found himself in the middle of a crowd. Cars had stopped behind one another and people were pushing forward. Drivers were leaning out of open windows and asking each other questions.

'He never gave me a chance,' the man explained to no one in particular. 'Came tearing round the corner right in the middle of the road – couldn't pull up – he skidded straight into me.'

'Do you live far from here?' a woman asked Brock.

'On the new estate,' Brock told her. He found it a great effort to speak at all.

'Here, that's Mary Brockson's little boy,' another woman called out.

'Where do they live?' the man asked.

'Churchill Street – 3 Churchill Street isn't it?' the same woman said.

Brock nodded his head.

The man wrote this down in a notebook he had taken from his pocket.

'I'm all right,' Brock said defiantly, and he wheeled his bike forward. The same woman picked up the saddle-bag and gave it to Brock. He put it under his free arm. People were still staring at him and they were talking about him too.

The driver walked back to his car. He leaned over the radiator and ran his fingers along the paintwork. Then, shaking his head, he climbed into the car and drove away. The stationary traffic began slowly to move after him. People continued to stare at Brock from the cars. A bus swung out and passed. Everybody was peering out at him. Brock looked at the ground. His hurt leg was making him limp. He hurried on, waited at the T-junction, and then crossed the road into the estate. He was shivering. He couldn't stop himself. It was as if he was cold and yet he wasn't cold. It was a warm evening now.

At the bottom of Churchill Street some small children were playing on the pavement. As he approached they stopped. They too stared at him.

'He's bust his bike,' a little girl said. The words rang in Brock's brain. He ignored their surprised faces, and went on. In front of him he could now see the gang on the green. Whitman had climbed up the lamp-post and the others were trying to pull him down. They were so engrossed, laughing and shouting, that at first they did not see Brock. Then Clayton said something, and the others all looked in his direction. Whitman slid down the lamp-post. They stood and watched him come closer and closer.

'Look at Titch,' Clayton said, as Brock approached. Scotty sniggered.

Brock couldn't make up his mind whether to walk straight past. He knew the gang could not help, knew what would happen, and yet he still wheeled his bike over to where they were standing.

'You been having a mud-bath?' Clayton asked.

Brock glanced down at his clothes. Mud covered the whole of the front of his jumper. It was no longer possible to see the picture of the bike.

'I had an accident,' Brock told them sadly. He longed for their sympathy, but did not receive it.

'We can see you've been in a smash,' Whitman observed dryly. He took the bike from Brock's hands and examined it all over, first the saddle, then the handlebars, then the pedal and finally the paintwork. He turned his detached gaze on Brock, and Brock flinched beneath his accusing eyes.

'In a thousand years, I'll never understand how you did it,' Whitman said. 'I built this with my own hands – from nothing I built it – part by part. It was a perfect piece of coordinated machinery. I had it a month. A thousand miles that bike travelled before it came to you and there wasn't a scratch or a mark on it.'

'Is it bad?' Scotty inquired, taking the saddle-bag from underneath Brock's arm.

'Bad!' Whitman exclaimed. 'In its present state, it's of use to neither man nor monkey.'

Brock felt overwhelmed by the torrent of words.

'I couldn't help it,' he sobbed, breaking into tears.

'Lovely, Titch, lovely,' Clayton sneered.

'Shut up,' Fagin snarled. He hadn't spoken before. 'One of you says another word and I'll do him.' Fagin glared aggressively, first at Whitman, then at Scotty and Clayton.

Nobody took up his challenge. A tense silence was broken by Clayton.

'Sorry, Titch – it was only a joke – we didn't really mean it.'

'Come on, Brock,' Fagin said kindly. 'I'll walk home with you.' He turned on Whitman and jerked the bike from his arms. Then he snatched the saddle-bag from Scotty.

Together, Fagin and Brock crossed the street. When they reached the end of Brock's house, Brock said, 'You'd better not come any further. I don't know what my dad will say.'

Fagin nodded, handed him the saddle-bag, and then walked away.

Brock wheeled the bike past the front window. Dad looked up absently but he didn't notice anything was wrong.

Brock leaned the bike against the wash-house, and then went in through the kitchen door. He stood, for several seconds, unwilling to enter the dining-room. But Dad had to be faced sometime. Dad had been right. Brock had to admit it. He would have been better to have stuck to 'The Tank'. The racing-bike had made him conceited. He wasn't any world champion, nor would he ever be. He was what he had always hated to admit to himself, somebody small for his age, who wasn't particularly good at anything.

Brock opened the dining-room door quietly. It swung open by itself. He stood there in the open doorway. Mum and Dad had finished their tea, and Dad was reading the newspaper. Brock couldn't see his face. Mum was watching the news on television. Mollie lay curled up on her lap. Mum was stroking the cat's ear. She must have sensed Brock's presence, because suddenly she raised her head and gave a frightened start. Mollie's ears pricked up and then she jumped from Mum's lap.

'John, don't come in like –' Mum started to say. Then she paused and gasped, 'John – Frank – our John – whatever's happened?' Dad lowered his newspaper abruptly. There was a startled expression on his face.

Brock stared down at the carpet and waited.

Dad had stood up and was coming towards him.

'John! Are you all right?' Dad asked.

Brock knew he wasn't angry. He could tell from the sound of his voice. Dad wasn't going to be annoyed with him.

'I bust my bike,' Brock said glumly. 'I had an accident and bust my bike.' And again he started to cry. Describing what had happened produced a flood of emotion in him. He couldn't control the tears. They just ran down his face and he could not stop them.

'Come and sit here, John,' Mum said.

Brock hobbled to the settee and sat beside her on the arm.

'You've hurt your leg!'

'It's nothing, Mum,' he told her. 'It's only where I fell, but it's all right really.'

Mum put her arms round him, and he laid his head against her shoulder.

Dad said he would go in the yard and look at the damage.

'It's my bike, Mummy,' he explained. 'It's not like the bike I had. It's not the same bike at all.'

'We'll put it right,' Mum comforted him. 'You wait and see. You won't be able to tell the difference.'

Dad came back in the room. There was a blank, worried expression on his face.

'He must have had an awful smack,' Dad said. 'I've put it away in the wash-house for tonight, John. You leave it till I come home from work tomorrow. We'll put things right together then.'

'Let me get some clean clothes,' Mum said. 'Give me that jumper – it'll all come off in the wash. Sit there and I'll bring you your tea. You'll feel better with food inside you.'

But he didn't feel better. And having to explain everything to Mum and Dad only upset him more. They asked him about the driver of the car, what he was like, but Brock couldn't remember anything about him, not even the colour of the car. He couldn't help thinking about the accident, how it would never have happened if he hadn't gone so fast. All he wanted was to be on his own. Though Mum and Dad couldn't have been kinder, he just wanted to be by himself.

After tea he went to his bedroom. He changed into his pyjamas, closed the window and drew the curtains. As he did so, there was a knock at the front door. Brock hoped it was nobody for him. He did not wish to see anybody; the prospect of ever having to meet people again filled him with dread. Most of all he dreaded meeting Mr and Mrs Bird for they had believed in his dreams. He wished to exclude the world completely from his own small room. He climbed into bed and pulled the clothes over his head. He burrowed his face into the sheets, moulded them around his body so that he was enclosed, as a young animal is in its nest. But he was not able to escape from his own thoughts. He could not shut them out. They invaded his mind, tormenting him. No matter how hard he tried, he could not escape from them.

Later Mum came upstairs and sat close to him on the bed and held his hand. She told Brock a policeman had called at the house. But nothing was wrong. He had only come to see that Brock was all right, that he hadn't been seriously hurt.

'Don't worry,' she consoled him. 'These things are never as bad as they seem at the time. In a year's time you'll have forgotten all about this. You'll look back and laugh at yourself.'

Brock didn't believe her, didn't believe that he would ever forget, or that he would ever laugh again. Although talking to her did help. He liked the story she told about when she'd been a little girl, and she'd longed for a horse more than anything in the world, and she'd never been able to have one. As she said, he might so easily have been killed on his bike, and then none of them would have had anything. She made him smile when she said that.

'That's better,' she comforted him, smiling back at him. 'Now you go to sleep and everything will be as right as rain in the morning.'

She straightened the bedclothes and then kissed

him good night. And despite all the worry and upset Brock did sleep almost immediately. Though he still felt sad there was a numbness in him, and as soon as he closed his eyes this numbness lost itself in sleep.

Fourteen

The weather had changed again. Once more summer had returned. The still air promised to turn into wavering heat, perhaps for the last time before autumn proper began.

Brock woke early with a dull pain in his leg. It was stiff and difficult to move. The moment he awoke he thought of the bike, and the remembrance of that twisted shape jolted him to consciousness.

Brock didn't want to get up. He was overcome with a heavy inertia. For a long while he lay in bed staring at the painting on the opposite wall. And he remembered how he had felt when he painted his bike. A shaft of sun had found its way through the curtains. Its sharp penetrating beam cast patterns of dappled light on the picture, picking out the tall figure in the track-suit and the bold black printing of the word BROCKSON.

Brock heard Dad get up, the radio was switched on, the kettle sang as it boiled, then Mum and Dad were talking. Everything was the same as it had always been. At five past eight Dad was off. A chair scraped on the floor downstairs. The kitchen door banged, tyres crunched on the driveway. Mum turned off the radio.

Outside a dog barked. Voices approached, hung and then faded on the summer air. A long way away a train urgently hurried by. The harsh sounds of cars and motor bikes came and went. Only the birdsong continually broke the quietness.

Finally there was nothing except the gradually increasing, shimmering heat. Still Brock lay in bed doing nothing.

At nine o'clock Mum brought him a cup of tea, a bowl of cornflakes and two slices of toast. He sat up in bed, took the tray from her and said, 'Thank you.'

Mum drew back the curtains. The room was flooded with sunlight.

'It's terribly stuffy in here,' Mum said. She opened the large window, and fastened the catch. Brock ate and drank mechanically. Mum was more cheerful than normal, and she spoke hurriedly.

'Dad says he'll bring home a tin of white paint and a new brush. You're to work together after tea.'

Brock nodded glumly. He stared at the tray. He couldn't bring himself to look her in the eyes.

'I'm going to town to do some shopping,' Mum

went on. 'We could look at some cycle shops if you would like to.'

Brock shook his head. He knew he was being difficult but he couldn't help it.

'Well, anyway, I'll bring back fish and chips for dinner. And I won't forget to ask for batter.'

Brock nodded again. He wasn't hungry, not even for fish and chips.

'I must rush or I'll miss the half past nine bus.'

'I'll be all right on my own,' Brock told her.

'Of course you will, John dear,' she said in that same comforting cheerful manner.

She came back upstairs, five minutes later, just to say cheerio. At last Brock had the house to himself. He climbed out of bed and went to the window. He watched Mum walk all the way down Churchill Street until she went round the corner and disappeared from sight. Those small children were playing outside their house. One of them had a tricycle and the others were taking it in turns to leap-frog over each other. Brock could hear their laughing voices quite clearly. He watched them for some time, until his attention was distracted by a white butterfly, which hovered beneath him.

Then he went back inside the room, sat on the bed and stared at the painting. The clock in the hall struck ten and then half past. Though he had no will for anything he forced himself to dress, and then he wandered about the house, aimlessly opening and shutting doors behind him. He turned on the radio and twiddled the knobs from one station to another.

After that he tried the television. The test card was on one of the channels. Brock sat in Dad's armchair and watched the lines on the picture waver up and down behind the glass.

Finally he turned that off too. Next he walked out into the street. It was deserted except for those small children. They must have recognized Brock, because they stopped playing and stared at him. Brock turned away and went back inside. He had thought the gang might have come to see him, but he was glad they hadn't.

He found himself in the kitchen. Mum had stacked the dirty breakfast dishes on the draining-board. Brock ran the water in the sink. He felt it with his hand and found it to be cold. He filled the electric kettle, plugged it in and pressed down the switch. Then he scraped the rinds of bacon from the plates and threw them in the waste bin. The kettle began to make its low shushing sound. Brock sorted the dishes into the washing-up bowl. He squeezed the plastic bottle of liquid. A green jet squirted into the sink. Steam rose from the spout of the electric kettle. Brock reached for the switch and at the same time poured boiling water over the dishes. He washed each plate, cup, saucer, knife, fork and spoon individually, and even more slowly he dried every article and placed it in its correct position.

It must have taken him almost an hour from start to finish. Yet when the task was completed he was at a loss what to do. He wiped his hands on the washing-up towel and as he did so the clock in the hallway struck twelve.

I'll have a quick look at my bike, Brock thought. Only a quick look to re-examine the damage.

Dad had put the bike at the back of the washhouse beside 'The Tank'. Brock had forgotten 'The Tank' existed. He lifted his new bike over the lawn-mower into the yard. Then he reached for the saddle-bag, which Dad had placed on his workbench. He was surprised to find that the scratched paintwork wasn't as bad as he had imagined it to be. And the handlebars and the saddle – they could be put right by loosening two bolts. The pedal was a different matter. It was badly twisted. But at the worst he could buy a new pedal. They couldn't cost very much money. And he had one pound and eighty-eight pence left from his savings. The paintwork would have to be left until Dad came home. The saddle and handlebars though – he could do those himself. He went to Dad's toolbox and took out the spanners. He started on the saddle because one of the spanners exactly fitted the bolt which tightened it. He exerted pressure – the bolt didn't move – he pushed harder – the spanner slipped off. Each time he tried the same thing happened.

Then he had the idea of turning the bike upside down. He'd have easier access to the bolt when the saddle was on the ground. But the same thing happened. He attempted kicking the spanner with his heel. When that didn't work he hit it with a hammer. Nothing would make the bolt move even a fraction of an inch. And the trouble was the bike wouldn't stay still – added to which the bolt was losing its shape. The spanner no longer exactly fitted the hexagonal top. Brock looked about him for somebody to help. Whitman would have loosened the bolt. But there were only two mothers with their prams, talking on the opposite side of the street. Brock knew he couldn't do it himself. He should have stopped and thought. The heat was overpowering, and his thick blue jumper was causing him to perspire heavily. But he didn't stop. An irresistible impulse forced him to go on.

In desperation he turned the bike right way up again and attempted to turn the nut which held the handlebars in place. It was the same story. Within five minutes the bolt head was burred and mis-shapen. Brock wiped the sweat from his face. He knew it was useless going on, but he had to try and try and try again. And the longer he tried the more agitated he became. At each straining pull he felt himself grow weaker and weaker, until finally he had to sit on the wash-shed step and rest.

He was becoming more and more despondent, when Judith opened the gate.

'Hello, Johnny,' she said, coming towards him. 'David's just told me about your accident.'

Brock showed her the damage. As she examined the bike Brock felt that same uncontrollable flood of emotion coming over him. Taking out his handkerchief he blew his nose. He didn't want her to see him crying and upset.

'It really is terribly bad luck,' she sympathized.

'Dad says he'll help me when he comes home from work,' Brock told her. 'But it won't make any difference. It'll never be the same.'

Judith tried to undo the bolts but she wasn't even as strong as Brock.

'I've just thought of something,' she said. 'I'll only be a minute.'

While Brock was waiting Mum came home with an overladen shopping bag. She hesitated in the yard, glanced quickly at the bike and then gave a tired sigh.

'Hello, John. You've no idea how busy town was,' she said. 'The fish and chips are in that paper bag. You're to come in at once before they go cold. And I don't know why you're wearing a woollen jumper on a day like this.'

Brock followed her into the kitchen. He divided the fish and chips and batter onto two plates, while Mum laid the table.

'That was very good of you to wash all those dishes,' Mum remarked.

'It wasn't anything,' Brock answered.

'Well, I appreciate it very much,' Mum told him, giving him a hug, and a kiss on the side of his face.

They had hardly sat down when the back gate slammed. Brock stood up, and wiped his mouth with his handkerchief.

'It's Judith. She wants to see me.'

'She can wait until you've finished your dinner.'

'But Mum!' Brock protested. 'It's important. It's about my bike.'

'You're to have your dinner first,' Mum told him.

Brock sat down again with a moan. While he was eating, he listened for footsteps approaching the kitchen door. He heard Judith speaking.

'Go on, David, please!'

'It was his own fault,' came Whitman's reply. 'In any case I want to start my new bike this afternoon.'

'You ought to mend it,' Judith went on. 'You do know that.' She was saying something else, but Brock couldn't catch the words. All he could hear was his own name mentioned again and again and again. Mum sprinkled vinegar on her chips. There was further muffled talking outside.

Finally Whitman shouted: 'All right – I suppose so.'

The back gate slammed and everything went quiet again. Mum hadn't spoken a word. She was looking straight in front of her. Brock took a drink of water and went on eating. He was almost finished.

A minute or so later the gate banged again. Something heavy was thrown on the ground. Mum had stood up and was making a pot of tea.

Brock placed his knife and fork in their correct position on the plate.

'Please may I leave the table?' he asked meekly.

'Certainly, dear,' Mum said, without turning round from the stove.

Brock opened the kitchen door and went out into the yard. Judith wasn't there any longer. Whitman's back was bent over the bike. He didn't look up, or even seem to notice that Brock was standing there. He had a spanner and was pulling on the seat bolt. His hands clenched round the spanner and strained. The bolt came loose.

'That's one done,' Whitman said. He had the seat back into position in less than five minutes.

Brock marvelled how his hands moved so quickly. He knew exactly where he was putting them.

'Hot out here,' Whitman observed, wiping his brow. 'Now you hold the front wheel while I straighten these handlebars.'

Brock did as he was told. Whitman was searching through his tool-kit when Fagin, Scotty and Clayton came through the gate. Fagin sat down on the dustbin and the other two stood beside him. Whitman gave a grunt of disgust and then found the right spanner.

'You're in my light,' he shouted. Fagin pushed Clayton in the back and indicated for him to move to one side. Whitman gave a satisfied nod and returned to the bike. It was exactly the same with the handlebars as it had been with the saddle. He had them back in their right place before Brock realized he had done it.

'Let's see this pedal,' Whitman said. 'You'll need to keep it in place with these pliers. Now hold it still. I won't hit your fingers.'

Brock shut his eyes as the hammer came down with a solid crack.

'Turn it over and we'll do the other side.'

Two more blows and it wasn't possible to tell the pedal had been twisted. Whitman was wonderful with bikes.

Next he took out a special spanner. With this he tightened several of the spoke nuts on the front wheel. Then he spun the wheel and held it away from his half-closed eye.

'Could be worse,' he remarked to himself. 'I'd better make a trial run for you.'

Whitman lifted the bike over the gate onto the road.

Brock's heart was in his mouth. What would Mum say? But really she couldn't object because Whitman was helping him.

All this time Scotty and Clayton hadn't moved. And Fagin sat beside them on the dustbin, smiling happily to himself.

When Whitman came back his face was flushed, and beads of sweat stood out on his forehead. He carried the bike to the anxious waiting figure of Brock.

'Seems to be fair enough. Now for this paintwork. Here's a piece of emery paper. Gently – rub it where the paint has come off – I'll fetch my spray gun.'

It's going to be all right, Brock thought. It's going to be all right after all.

'Not like that,' Whitman shouted, when he returned. 'Here, give it to me before you ruin it. Now open this tin of paint.'

'What with?' Brock asked him.

'With your teeth, what do you think?'

Brock couldn't help laughing. He laughed happily with a kind of relief. Whitman was really funny sometimes.

Brock found a screwdriver and opened the tin of paint.

Ten minutes later it was finished. There was only the saddle-bag to be put back in place, and that was done in a matter of seconds.

'Thank you ever so much – David,' Brock said. He could not remember calling Whitman by his Christian name before.

'No need for thanks,' Whitman answered, with an unusually friendly smile. 'One thing, don't ride it for two hours, because the paint won't be dry till then. Now you will remember!'

Brock promised he would.

Whitman packed away his tools, took one last, fond look at the bike, and then he was gone.

Brock rushed inside. He found Mum tidying his bedroom.

'Wasn't it good of him?' Brock said. 'It really was good of him.'

Mum didn't say anything except to ask whether any of the paint had gone on the yard, but Brock knew she was pleased.

He went back downstairs and invited the gang into the house. It was so hot outside. They all agreed it would be best to have a game of Monopoly. Brock got out the box and they arranged everything on the coffee table in the living-room. It reminded Brock of his birthday, which seemed a lifetime away, though it had only been last month.

The game that afternoon was unlike any other game they had played. Nobody grabbed for the egg-cup, and there were no arguments about the number of spaces that had to be moved. Strangely, Brock won, and Fagin was runner-up. Scotty and Clayton had almost no money at the end. They all helped to pack away and as Brock replaced the lid, Clayton said suddenly,

'I'm sorry about last night, Titch – I mean, Brock.'

'You said you were sorry last night,' Brock told him.

'I wasn't sorry last night,' Clayton answered. 'But I am now – truthfully I am.'

There was a long painful silence. They were too embarrassed to look at one another.

'You can all have a ride on my bike,' Brock said gently. 'If you would like to.'

'Will it be all right?' Fagin asked.

Brock hesitated and then answered.

'It's my bike and I say it's all right.'

Brock led them into the yard, and wheeled the bike on to the road.

Fagin touched the paintwork with the ends of his fingers.

'It's perfectly dry,' he said.

'You have first go, Franklin,' Brock told him.

'Yes, if you say so,' Fagin answered. 'Thank you very much, Brock.' There was a glint of pride in his eyes as he took the bike from Brock's hands.

Brock experienced a feeling of jealousy at somebody else riding his bike, but he pushed the resentment from his mind.

'It's a great bike,' Fagin said, when he came back.

'I'll go last,' Scotty volunteered.

Brock handed the bike to Clayton, and as he did so he happened to look up. Mum was watching them from his bedroom window. Brock stared at her straight in the eyes. Her mouth curled in a faint smile, and then she turned away with the blanket which was in her hands.

'I wish I had a bike like this,' was Clayton's comment, when he returned to Brock.

Scotty said Brock was the luckiest person in the world.

Brock wasn't certain he agreed with him. After the gang had left, Brock sat on the sofa and watched a cricket match on the television, though he did not watch it properly, because he wasn't aware of the score, nor even who was playing. For more than an hour he gazed vacantly in front of him. His body was tired and limp. He was neither happy nor sad, but rather in a state of quiet contentment. After all the conflict he had experienced, he now felt completely at peace. He had no wish for anything.

Dad came home at a quarter to six. Brock heard Mum telling him everything in the kitchen.

'So we won't need this tin of paint,' Dad said,

smiling as he entered the dining-room. They all had tea together. Mollie was asleep on the sofa. Mum switched off the television and then she asked Dad if there was any news from the office. While he was talking Mum poured out the tea. Brock had a warm happy feeling inside him as he sat and listened. Mollie woke up, arched her legs and shook herself. Then she jumped onto Mum's lap.

'I was thinking,' Dad said, turning to Brock. 'I was thinking – we could go for a ride tonight – on our bikes.'

'Oh, yes, I should like to,' Brock replied.

'That is, if you haven't planned anything with your friends?'

'No, nothing,' Brock told him. 'Nothing at all.'

'In that case we ought to be making a start,' Dad said.

'Let me fetch John's new jumper, Frank,' Mum said. 'It'll have dried by now.'

Brock put it on and they were ready.

The sun was low over the rooftops. After the heat of the day the evening air was cool and refreshing. The gang were standing under the lamp-post on the green when Brock and Dad wheeled their bikes onto the street. Dad mounted and rode in front. Brock quickly caught up with him. Side by side they approached the gang.

'Good evening, boys,' Dad called out.

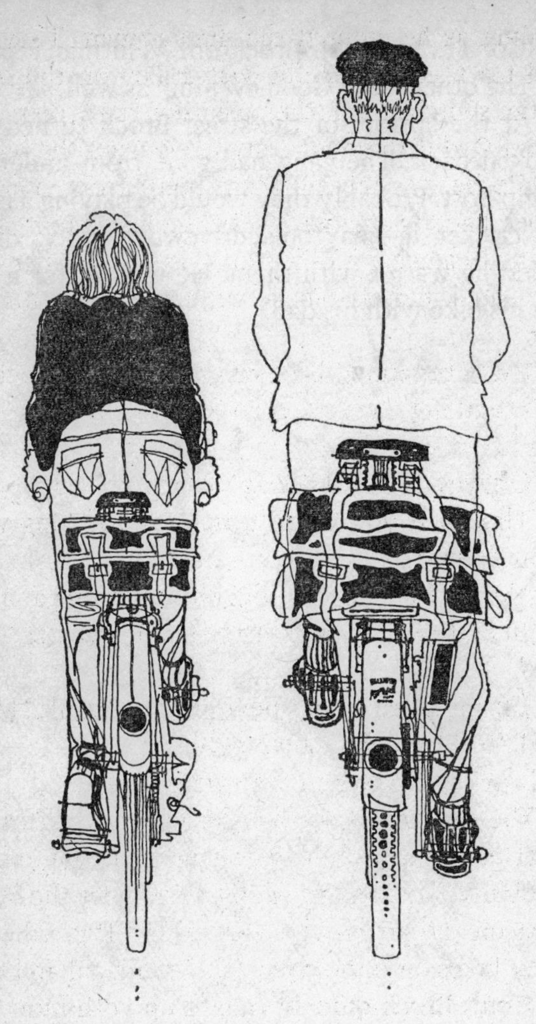

'Good evening, Mr Brockson,' Whitman replied. The others said 'Good evening' as well.

At the bottom of the street Brock turned and looked back. The gang had gone from under the lamp-post. Probably they would be playing a game of cricket in Clayton's driveway. Brock didn't mind he wasn't with them. He was off for a ride on his bike with his dad.

Some other Puffins

THE FROG REPORT

Benjamin Lee

If Uncle Leopold hadn't offered Jonathan fifteen pence a chapter, this book would never have been written, very probably. Which would have been a great pity.

For Jonathan's sake, we won't give away too much, but the background is that Daniel, Jenny and Jonathan live in a quiet seaside town called Dullington Bay on the South Coast. One night while their parents are in London, they go for a walk along the cliff top. What goes wrong is serious enough, but it's only the beginning of a series of other things. However, that's Jonathan's story. Quite where the frogs come into it you'll discover in due course. But it's fun and exciting too.

THUNDER AND LIGHTNINGS

Jan Mark

Victor knew more about aeroplanes than anyone Andrew had ever met. His room was full of models and pictures. His lamp was especially dimmed so that it looked like a bomber's moon. Andrew was fascinated by Victor's devotion to planes, but as their friendship grew, Andrew became more and more worried about what would happen to Victor when he discovered that his beloved Lightnings were to be replaced by Jaguars ...

TIGER IN THE BUSH

Nan Chauncy

The Lorenny family lived in a secret valley, hidden so deep in the mountains that no map markers had discovered it, where the rarest creatures lived safe from the menaces of hunters or the curiosity of scientists. When Dad and the others were away on a prospecting trip, and Badge and his mother were left in charge of the farm, two friendly strangers appeared and asked to set up camp, and, fatally warming to their friendship and interest, Badge confided to them that the rarest animal of all, the nearly-extinct Tasmanian tiger, could still be seen in the valley. The moment he had spoken, he senses the disaster and, desperate to find a way to undo the damage before the wild and splendid creature was outlawed or killed, by too much interest, he embarked on the only plan he could think of, one that was to lead him into real danger ...

MINNOW ON THE SAY

Philippa Pearce

The floods brought the canoe to the foot of David's garden, and the canoe brought David to Adam Codling, its proper owner. That was how David and Adam became friends, scraped and varnished the boat, and named her *Minnow*. Then they made plans for how they should use her.

Of course, they could just paddle her up and down the river, the Say, and picnic and climb the willows and fish, but Adam wanted to do more than that – he intended to use the *Minnow* to find the family treasure which his ancestor had hidden centuries before. But time was running out, and with the family in such financial trouble there was little chance that Adam would be there next summer to paddle the *Minnow* on the Say.

Heard about the Puffin Club?

. . . it's a way of finding out more about Puffin books and authors, of winning prizes (in competitions), sharing jokes, a secret code, and perhaps seeing your name in print! When you join you get a copy of our magazine, *Puffin Post*, sent to you four times a year, a badge and a membership book.

For details of subscription and an application form, send a stamped addressed envelope to:

The Puffin Club Dept A
Penguin Books Limited
Bath Road,
Harmondsworth
Middlesex UB7 ODA

and if you live in Australia, please write to.

The Australian Puffin Club
Penguin Books Australia Limited
P.O. Box 527
Ringwood
Victoria 3134